Embracing Your *Authentic* SELF

Women's Intimate Stories Of
Self-Discovery & Transformation

Published by Inspired Living Publishing, LLC.
P.O. Box 1149, Lakeville, MA 02347

ISBN-13: 978-0-9845006-2-8
ISBN-10: 0-9845006-2-6

Library of Congress Control Number: 2011935552

www.inspiredlivingpublishing.com
(508) 265-7929

Cover and Layout Design: Rachel Dunham, www.hummingbirdcreativeconcepts.com

Editor: Bryna René, Aphrodite, Inc. www.wordsbyaphrodite.com

Printed in the United States.

DEDICATION

This book is dedicated to...

Every woman who, in honoring the calling of the still, small voice within, has taken her first steps on the winding path to authenticity.

Every woman who bravely chooses to brush aside fear and self-doubt, and peel back the layers that hide or darken her divine light.

Every woman further along in her journey who lights the way for others to follow. Thank you for being a beacon.

And also to...

Niki, my beautiful daughter, who embodies the qualities of an authentic woman with grace and compassion—and who, in just a few months, will bless the world with a child of her own. You are, and always will be, my shining star.

The multitude of extraordinary women who have come into my life over the last twenty years. Your wisdom, bravery, and generosity of spirit have touched me beyond words. My greatest wish is that I may light the way for others as you have for me.

My coauthors, who entrusted their stories to me and allowed me to share their spirit nets with the world.

The extraordinary team of women with whom I am honored, blessed, and humbled to work to bring this project to life: Rachel Dunham, the creative visionary behind the visual graphics of this book (and all my brands), who continues to amaze me with her innate gifts; Kim Turcotte, Project Manager and owner of Grow Your Divine Business, who has a gift for breaking down my big dreams into bite-sized pieces and bringing them to life; Bryna René, Editor for Inspired Living Publishing, who brings the essence and truth of each story to light with ease and grace.

And finally, to...

The countless women around the world who continue to embrace and support my mission to inspire women to live deeper, more authentic, inspired lives. I am humbled by gratitude, and I love you all.

PRAISE FOR
Embracing Your Authentic Self

"Living authentically takes courage, conviction, and self-love, and that is exactly what *Embracing Your Authentic Self* inspires readers to experience. It reaches into the hearts of readers and empowers them to live a life that is lovingly detached from the opinions of others and aligned with their own deepest truth. I invite you to embrace this book and dare to be yourself."
– **Laura V. Grace,** author of *Gifts of the Soul* and *The Intimate Soul*

"In a world where far to many of us are wearing the mask of who or what we are 'expected' to be, when we are gifted with the authentic truth there is no denying its presence. The stories gathered here from women who have traveled the path to burn away the mask and step into their true nature are inspiring, uplifting, motivational, and filled with the power of their own deep spirit. Take the time to really read these messages—both the ones on the page, and those that emanate powerfully from between the lines! Laugh, cry, and be open to what it means to be who you *really* are!"
– **Amethyst Wyldfyre,** Navigational Guide and Divine Destiny Mastery Mentor for Messengers

"I just finished reading *Embracing Your Authentic Self* and I couldn't put it down. It is a book like none other I have read. The depth, honesty, and courage of each woman's story brought tears to my eyes and blessed me in many ways. Their real-life stories of transformation…will help readers go within to discover and embrace their authentic selves. The journaling questions at the end of each chapter are very helpful. If you want to be inspired and find your authentic self, this is the book for you. I know it will change your life, just as it has mine."
– **Pat Hastings,** Author of *Simply a Woman of Faith*

"I felt a deep spark within me as I read one of the stories, calling me to deepen my faith in the force that guides my life… [This book] reactivated a sense of wonder inside of me at the power that comes when you're stripped of your fears."
– Fia-Lynn Crandall

"*Embracing Your Authentic Self* is filled with stories that share surprising truths. As a reader, I felt so honored to be let in to these authors' inner worlds—their deep experiences, the little lies they told, their "coming out" with the truth. Their healings helped me heal, their light upon their darkness shed light upon my own. I enjoyed their triumphs more deeply because of the vulnerabilities they share. Linda Joy and Inspired Living Publishing have created another treasure. If you're looking for a great book for a friend (or yourself) this is it. I look forward to sharing it."
– **Lisa Tener,** book writing coach and author

"Having experienced her own transformational journey, Linda Joy recognizes the healing power of a journey shared. She has gathered together a stunning array of women, each with a life-changing story that will inspire, encourage, and empower you to embrace your authentic self."
– **Elizabeth Harper,** color intuitive, visionary artist and author of *Wishing: How to Fulfill Your Heart's Desires*

"Linda Joy is a woman standing authentically, embracing others in sharing their stories and inspiring them to step into joyful living. As this book goes out to the world, the inner joy shared will inspire others to live more truthfully. Thus Linda's mission, inspiring joyful living, will multiply at a miraculous rate."
– **Kate Michaels,** Core Alignment Specialist and Author

"Linda Joy has done it again! *Embracing Your Authentic Self* is a book that is sure to inspire, heal, and transform women's lives all over the world. Don't miss it!"
– **Terri Amos-Britt,** author of *The Enlightened Mom* and founder of TheEnlightenedMom.com

"[In *Embracing Your Authentic Self*] Linda Joy has brought some amazing women together to share their poignant moments of self-discovery. As you read these stories you will be touched by how they worked through the difficulties in their lives. Women are being called to discover their authentic selves, and as you witness their transformations you will know that you also can take the necessary steps to develop your full potential."
– **Kris Steinnes,** author of the award winning book *Women of Wisdom: Empowering the Dreams and Spirit of Women*

"This book is 100% authentic. Filled with wisdom, depth, insight, and a beauty that will empower and move you to believe, honor, and trust in your own inner beauty. Expect to be inspired to live your life to the fullest, and to be exactly who you are. A heartwarming and hope-filled read!"

– **Linda Pestana,** author of *Voices of the Heart*

FOREWORD
by Nicola Phoenix
SPIRITUAL PSYCHOLOGIST

*L*ife is an ever-evolving journey of grace. However, there are points within this journey when we find ourselves questioning how we spend our sacred moments. Looking back, these moments stand out as turning points in our personal transformation, as if we were being coaxed to see so much more—yet at the time, as we faced despair, fear, anger or disappointment, we may not have realized the importance of these valuable life lessons. Too busy coping with what was happening, looking for answers to ease our suffering, we may have been unable to see the gift of transformation that was occurring.

As the world becomes ever more goal-focused, we condition ourselves to see the end result as the "win," and often totally disregard the essential stages that we needed to experience in order to transform ourselves. The mindset of win or lose, success or failure, has become so ingrained that, during the in-between stages of the journey itself, we continually wish to be *elsewhere*. However, as you will notice in each of the inspiring stories in this book, the present moment, however uncomfortable it may be, holds the fertile environment for us to wake up to our authentic self and its Divine expression in *every* present moment, not just the "winning" ones.

As we shed the illusions of who we thought we were, the roles we thought we had to play, and our beliefs about our own self-worth, we see that the greatest connection and most rewarding relationship possible emerges: our relationship with ourselves. Stepping into a more conscious way of being provides a platform for immense growth, because a life with peace in our hearts and fulfilment in our every expression is our birthright.

The conditioning of your informative childhood years, and the experiences that have led you to where you stand today, may not support this idea. In fact, this idea may be in conflict with your existing belief system. So often, we are taught to look outside of ourselves for the Divine; to nature, or to a vision of God which is so great that to think of ourselves as "divine" seems almost a crime. We build images of ourselves as separate from the great and incredible, and our low self-worth reflects this disempowered state.

As we begin to wake up, however, we see that we are like pieces in a huge jigsaw puzzle: part of the Universe, not apart from it. Once we realize this, we no longer need to separate ourselves from the incredible, from each other, or from our state of radiance. The same spark of magnificence which flows through each and every one of us is the expression of the Divine energy that resonates through the Universe. We do not need to change to please other people, or try to be like someone else, or spend endless time creating an identity that will make us look or feel "good enough." The fact that we have shown up to experience this divine life in all its glory is enough to make us matter.

You may discard these words because part of you is still holding on to the old idea that you are not good enough. Yet a part of you—one that does not need to be labelled or investigated—is still reaching out for something more, saying, "I can't stay with these feelings of suffering any more. I am going to shrink inside unless I spread my wings and start being the person I have the capacity to be." Honoring this feeling, and building your life to resonate with this expression of you, is a wonderful way to embrace your authentic self.

The journey toward allowing this divine essence to be expressed starts the moment we realize that there could be *another way*. The paradox of suffering is that at times we need it to help us to wake up, yet once we are awoken we need to be brave enough to step away from it. By opening this book, you acknowledge that you have already arrived at this place; that you are ready to leave behind negative feelings too heavy for a being who was sent here to shine. Each inspiring story that you will read, every message of learning and point of reflection, will assist you in realizing your capacity to live authentically from your heart's wishes and express your unique message to this world.

My work is to teach people to see in themselves what I see in them so clearly: that they are perfect right now, where they are. If a book were to be the demonstration of this valuable lesson in life, you are holding it in your hands. These stories prove that we can move beyond the limitations and habitual self-criticisms of the past in order to find ease, comfort, and true joy in the present. Storytelling gives us permission to see what is possible—how, from one spark of questioning, a feeling or an idea can be turned into reality. Use this book as a springboard to share your stories with other women, and continue the remarkable work that Linda Joy has created.

Be in touch with your feelings. Honor them: they are sacred. They are your divine calling, and therefore they are authentically you. More than anything else, you deserve to be happy and fulfilled. That is why you were put here in the first place.

With love on your journey,

Nicola Phoenix

Spiritual Psychologist
London, England

TABLE OF

CHAPTER THREE — SPIRITUAL AWAKENING

CHAPTER FOUR — AUTHENTIC FAMILIES

CHAPTER FIVE — GROWING INTO YOUR AUTHENTIC SELF

CHAPTER SIX—SHEDDING THE "SHOULDS"

CHAPTER SEVEN— BACK TO BUSINESS: AUTHENTICITY IN ACTION

CHAPTER EIGHT—MAKING THE CONNECTION

INTRODUCTION
by Linda Joy
PUBLISHER

"You can see the core of yourself—the hidden reassure of
yourself—in a teaching story, in my story, in your story,
and all other stories"
- Gangaji, Spiritual Teacher

*F*rom the earliest times, storytelling has been one of the most important tools used to inspire, empower, teach, and comfort. In the sharing of stories, family members passed on the wisdom and values of previous generations, and communities passed on the culture and history of their people.

As little girls, we were enraptured by the stories our parents told us as they tucked us into bed at night. Whether fairy tale classics or stories of their own childhoods, these stories were a vehicle for us to envision possibility, experience the power of imagination, and believe that anything was possible.

You are a storyteller. We all are. Each time you share your daily experiences or your intimate hopes, dreams and fears with your girlfriends, you are a storyteller. Each time you sit around the dinner table, reminiscing about your childhood with your family, you are a storyteller. The stories we tell one another—and ourselves—are powerful tools to communicate our unique experiences and beliefs; the essence of who we are.

In the book, *Who Says? Essays of Pivotal Issues in Contemporary Storytelling*, Anthropologist Robin Ridington proposes that "stories are a spirit net." The moment a life experience occurs it becomes a part of our essence (spirit net); eventually, through storytelling, that experience is sent down as part of our collective history, and passed from generation to generation.

When I first read those five powerful words, "stories are a spirit net," I felt a connection deep within my soul. They fully captured my personal mission and the work I do in the world.

I use the term "authentic storytelling" to describe the styles and types of stories I strive to share through my publishing projects. I have always been drawn to the personal, intimate stories of women who have not only lived through unique and sometimes painful life experiences, but who came out the other side armed with wisdom, love, and the hearts of warrior women.

Authentic storytelling showcases the essence of the storyteller or writer as she steps forward to share her triumphs and tragedies, lessons and insights. They are shared with the intent to empower, inspire, and guide the reader toward the realization that she too has the innate power to overcome any perceived obstacle and achieve the life of her dreams.

There comes a time in every woman's life when she experiences a yearning from within; it is a restlessness, a calling from the deepest recesses of her heart. She feels this gentle nudge, and strains to hear the words that are whispered to her. But she won't be fully be able to appreciate what she hears until she walks the often bitter road of self-discovery, slowly peeling back layer after layer of false masks and limiting beliefs until the separation between herself and her soul no longer exists. On that day, she will come face-to-face with her authentic self, her truest incarnation. The two can then become one, embracing, dancing, celebrating the homecoming.

My story is very much like those of the other amazing women whose authentic storytelling is featured on the pages of *Embracing Your Authentic Self.* Who knows—my story may even be yours!

On a beautiful spring day in 2001, I experienced a transformational moment which forever altered the trajectory of my life and launched me on a journey of self-discovery which continues to this day. This journey, like those of the heroines of our favorite fairy tales, took me down the winding roads of Self-Esteem, through the valleys of Pain and Despair, and across the breathtaking mountains of Hopes and Dreams, as I sought the greatest treasure of all: my authentic self, the self who has always been there, quietly waiting for me to bring her out of the darkness.

Every heroine needs tools to help her along in her quest. The written word has been, and continues to be, one of the most powerful tools in my transformational toolkit. Words have empowered me throughout my journey from single welfare mom to best-selling inspirational publisher. The wisdom contained within the books that became my friends and companions gave me the solace and inspiration I needed as impetus for change. Always, when my days seemed darkest, a word, a sentence, a paragraph would jump off a page at me, and provide me with the fuel I needed to keep moving forward.

In this book, you will meet twenty-six extraordinary women whose stories of self-discovery and transformation reveal the truth of their experiences. Warrior women all, each has come through her personal quest having released the unwanted baggage of the past, and given herself permission to heal. Now, these women are standing tall and shining their brilliant lights for others who are ready to begin their own journeys. As they welcome you into their spirit nets, they will show you how you, too, might choose to view life through the lens of possibility, and embrace the shimmering treasure that is your authentic self.

3

My greatest wish for you is that you discover on these pages the message your heart needs and your soul longs for, and that this message takes you one step (or many) further along the path to your authenticity. Take the time to work with the themes in each story using the "Tune In to Your Authentic Self" journaling prompts after each story; let the questions be like candles in a dark room, guiding your way toward understanding.

It doesn't matter where you've been, or what setbacks you've experienced; just like the heroines of great fairy tales, we all have the potential inside us to live happily ever after. Tomorrow is a new day, after all, and you have the power to choose the lens through which you will view it.

May your story be a great one, and may all your paths be *inspired!*

With love,

Linda Joy

Publisher,
Inspired Living Publishing, LLC

CHAPTER ONE

THE POWER OF
Truth

8

Seeing is Believing

Saskia Röell

I stare into the fire. I am moments away from standing right in the middle of it. I am beyond fear. I tremble uncontrollably and even my jaws clatter. Nobody pays any attention to me. The orange flames shoot like arrows into the New Mexico sky. In their quest to reach the sky, they sizzle as they passionately meet the falling snowflakes for a wet kiss.

"Get out of here!" my fearful self says. "You're out of your mind!" Little did I know that I had to be a bit out of my mind in order to survive the sacred ritual that was about to begin.

9

I thought good karma would save me from having to walk through the fire, as my flight was leaving before the fire walk. But I was wrong. They rescheduled the fire walk. I tried to talk them out of it, assured them that they didn't have to reschedule just because of me. "My time will come," I told them with great confidence. But they didn't listen. They were glad to reschedule so I could be there. "You wouldn't want to miss it for anything in the world" they said.

I couldn't have disagreed more. But somehow, somewhere, deep inside me, I heard Soul's whisper: "Stay," was all she said. I wondered if she realized that I have a body made of flesh and blood.

I will soon find how good my karma is: the only way out is through. There is no escape. My time has come.

The people laugh and sing while they help build up the fire until it's as big as it needs to be. We're told to pick a log and throw it into the fire. Our logs represent our issues. The idea is that the fire will transmute our issues, but right now, I couldn't care less about any of my issues except one: how to walk across this fire. I look for the biggest piece of wood I can find and, with a nonchalant swing, throw it into the blaze. I honestly don't think the fire can transmute my fear, unless I figure out how to stand on my bare feet in the middle of the hot burning coals.

I shiver and look into the starlit sky above me. If I didn't know better, I'd think I was in paradise. The sound of a pack of howling coyotes brings me back to reality. For once, they don't scare me. If I can face walking through a fire, coyotes don't bother me one bit.

Then I hear the instructor say we're almost ready to go. She asks us to come with her into the meditation building. It doesn't take her long to explain. "Seeing is believing," she says. "It's mind over matter." I'm upset that the instructions are so sparse. We're told to ask our higher selves *if* we can walk today. And, if so, we need to ask for a message. So I ask, and I hear Soul's immediate answer: "Yes, you can walk the fire three or four times, but float weightlessly and soar like an eagle. Make sure you walk with ease and grace." She repeats the words "ease and grace" three times. Did I hear that correctly? I couldn't have made it up. *No,* I think. *One crossing will be plenty for me.*

The last thing the instructor adds is that we cannot walk by tapping into our courage. We can only walk if our higher self gives us the green light. I am at a loss because usually my courage *is* my strength.

A minute later, I'm standing at the edge of the fire. I'm frozen in place. Everyone else walks. As they go back and forth, I decide to give myself permission not to go. I talk myself out of it. I tell myself I think it's very brave to be the last one standing. Then, something happens. I become mesmerized, fascinated by the magnetic pull of the hot coals. I can't take my eyes off the people who scream at the top of their lungs and run over the fire. Seeing is believing, yet I gasp in disbelief at what is happening. One after another, people walk quickly across the fire. And suddenly, without thinking about the instructions from my Soul, I decide to cross to the other side, too.

I'm in a rush. I no longer want to be the last one standing, and there I go. But my fearful self is in charge. I forget my Soul's eagle image. I forget to walk with ease and grace. Instead, I run as if my life depends on getting to the other side. After I'm across, I feel a burning pain in my feet. When I look, there are big blisters on each foot. Now I feel ashamed and stupid that I didn't listen to my Soul. I should have walked with ease and grace. *Did I fail Soul's test? Do I dare to trust her?* My feet are in bad shape. So am I.

I stand motionless in the snow for a few minutes. I take my time to contemplate, but deep down I know my truth. If I want to walk the path of the Soul, I'd better believe what Soul says. I have to cross again. *Who would walk through fire with burnt soles?* But this is a crucial moment. To walk my talk, I have to listen to my Soul and risk my feet. I have no choice. I've trusted Soul before and now I'm being asked to do it again. Will I make it through?

I take a breath and deliberately put my right foot into the fire. I walk. With each step, I mumble the words "ease and grace." Slowly, I set one foot after the other. I begin to float. I spread my wings and soar above the fire. My body feels weightless. I walk three more times. It even feels as though the hot coals soothe and heal my wounds. With each step, my feet sink deeper into the coals, which now feel like soft cotton balls.

After three crossings, I stop. I know I've passed the test. My feet tingle and my heart bursts with joy.

That night, as I lie in bed, I glow from head to toe. I think about that crucial moment of choice. I had been asked to trust Soul's guidance on a much deeper level than ever before, and I'd almost lost all of what I'd learned so far. That was close.

I imagine myself as an eagle soaring above my life. I see the times I've courageously followed the footsteps of my Soul, how I've learned to listen and leap—not once, but many times. In that process of listening and leaping, I lost my best friend, my marriage, my job, my country, my pets, and my country club life—all of which I'd dearly loved. But I gained the man of my dreams, five beautiful children, the house of my dreams in the land of my dreams, and work I love. It hasn't been easy, and I had to go far outside my comfort zone. But I did it. I shed my baggage and let go of my deepest fears. I made extraordinary choices and met extraordinary challenges. I listened, no matter what, and miracles happened.

I smile as I fall asleep, thinking of Soul. When I wake up the next morning, I look at my feet and laugh. As our instructor said, "Seeing is believing." The blisters are gone. The soles of my feet are healthy and pink. I feel so alive.

My Soul smiles back.

TUNE IN TO YOUR *Authentic* SELF

Have you ever done something that terrified you? What was the result?

_____

_____

_____

_____

Think of occasions when you've trusted your instincts, your faith, or messages from your Soul. How did those situations resolve? Would they have turned out differently had you ignored your internal wisdom?

_____

_____ 13

_____

_____

When she woke up the morning after her fire walk, Saskia's feet were completely healed. Have you ever experienced a miracle in the wake of trusting your Soul?

_____

_____

_____

_____

14

The Miracle Inside

Aysha Strausbaugh

"Miracles happen every day. One just did"
- Kate Michels

It was New Years Eve, and all I could do was cry.

I was on the phone with my life coach, Kate, crying so hard I could barely talk. "I will never have a relationship with a man," I was saying. "I am so sick of all the lies, and the cheating, and the games men play. I mean, what is wrong with me? Am I not attractive? What do I have to change about myself so I can have a good relationship?"

She was quiet for a moment. Then, she asked, "What kind of relationship do you want to have?"

"That's a great question," I thought. In my sad state of mind, I kept spinning over and over in my head what I would never have. Did guys only want sex from me? Was there something wrong with me? I was so tired of being alone, but I never felt anything *but* alone.

Then, it came to me. "I want a relationship I can trust," I said.

As soon as I focused on what I wanted, rather than what men wanted from me, the conversation shifted. I hung up the phone feeling uplifted, and made what would turn out to be one of the most important decisions of my life.

I was going to go out and have fun this New Year's Eve.

My friend Lucy and I decided to go to a "Pimp and Ho" theme party at a club. I ran out to the store to get my costume. I was going to look *good*, I decided. I put on sexy stripper boots, and pinned some clip-in hair extensions in my short blond hair. Lucy came over, dressed as my pimp, and we had a fabulous dinner together, talking about where this night could take us. After all, you never know who you're going to meet at these kinds of events.

Filled with the new power of what *I* wanted, I felt beautiful and sexy. I wasn't out to impress a man: I was out to have fun. As we walked into the club, I could feel everyone looking at me. My inner goddess was shining, and I let her. I strutted around in those boots with a confidence I hadn't felt in years.

On the dance floor, I moved like I'd never moved before, totally free. Even though I was in costume, that night I embraced the truth in me, the dancer inside. I wasn't scared, wondering if I would meet a man who would love me; instead, I loved who I was in that moment, and accepted all of me. I felt whole and complete, and it showed in every fiber of my being.

That night, the universe delivered all that I wanted. The intense chemistry that evening did not end at the club. It was met by others who recognized the beauty inside of me.

I called Kate and told her the whole story. "I had so much fun," I said. "Both men and women noticed how beautiful I was. They all wanted to dance with me, just to be in my presence. It was so surreal!" I told her about my encounter later in the evening, and how I never thought twice about anything I was doing. I had embraced the flow of the night, and let myself be danced into a world of excitement and ecstasy.

The backlash hit me two days later, like the floods that come over tropical islands, destroying all that is beautiful and alive. I could not believe myself. What had I done? How could I have taken that kind of risk? What was I thinking? Had I been thinking at all?

Again, the negative thoughts were spinning in my head. My body started to tremble with fear. I called Kate right away. She listened to me for a while, then said, "How can you go from such a place of beauty to such a place of fear?"

Those words stopped me. I was reminded of how special and beautiful my New Year's Eve had been, and how amazing I'd felt. I had to put my fears aside and make a choice to live in the beauty of what I'd experienced, rather than fearing what might come of it.

What came of that evening was a miracle.

On January 29, I took my friend Gina's hip hop class at the gym. My body type is thin; my tummy is flat. But that night, I felt really bloated. After class, I talked to Gina about it. She grinned. "Girl, either you gotta poop like crazy, or you're pregnant!"

I just laughed. There was no way I could be pregnant. That dream had died for me a long time ago. I'd been diagnosed with "unexplained infertility" several years before, while married to a Muslim man and living in the United Arab Emirates. When we discovered, after three years of marriage, that I was infertile, he informed me that he was going to take another wife. I couldn't have a child, therefore I was useless. I'd thought our relationship was built on love, but it didn't feel that way anymore. I wasted away to a mere one hundred and four pounds, and my skin started looking sallow and old. I felt as if my life was over. I had all the material things I wanted, but the man I loved was setting me aside for someone else.

In 2001, I found the courage to divorce my husband and return to the United States. I spent the next several years learning to love myself again. In an attempt to find the cause of my infertility, I had surgery, after which I was diagnosed with endometriosis. I bought my own house, opened a salon, and started working with Kate. I decided that I was going to be happy, baby or not. But what I wanted was a relationship I could trust.

The night after my conversation with Gina, I could barely sleep. The next morning, hardly daring to hope, I drove to the store and bought a pregnancy test. As soon as my pee hit the window, the positive result popped up.

I was thirty-eight years old, and I was going to have a baby!

I called my mom. "Just when you thought I couldn't shock you anymore," I said, "I'm going to do it right now."

Now, you have to understand that I've done some pretty shocking stuff in my life. I decided for a brief period in my troubled teenage years that it was my calling to be a stripper. I ran off to join the circus. I converted to Islam to marry the man who eventually set me aside. So it was perfectly understandable that my mom's response was, "What now, Aysha?"

Then, I hit her with the news. "I'm pregnant! I'm going to have a baby!"

"You're kidding!" My mom laughed. After all, this was going to be her first grandchild.

I loved every single moment of my pregnancy. I have never felt better in my life—and it all came about because I embraced the beauty of who I am on the inside, and let it shine through to the world. Only by loving myself completely could I find the miracle that was now growing inside my body.

Of course, there were fears that came and went during my pregnancy journey. I recognized them, and gently let them go. After all, God was not going to give me this miracle baby and then drop me on my butt! The birthing room was filled with amazing people—women I didn't necessarily see on a regular basis, but who took time out of their lives to witness my miracle come into the world. When Chloie arrived on September 26, she was welcomed with so much love. The moment she was born, I told her, "You are such a blessing." While she lay on my chest for the first time, I could hear my friends calling everyone we knew, announcing her arrival.

My Chloie has inspired me to share everything I've learned with others. Although the journey wasn't easy, I am so grateful that I didn't give up five minutes before my miracle. Today, my dream is for other women to recognize the miracles inside, and let them grow.

TUNE IN TO YOUR *Authentic* SELF

When was the last time you allowed your inner Goddess to shine? What was the result?

_____

_____

_____

_____

Often, we second-guess our authentic actions, especially when they seem to serve no purpose other than making us feel good. Looking back, have your "unconventional" actions served a purpose you couldn't see at the time?

_____

_____

_____

_____

By stepping out of her fear, Aysha made room for a miracle to be born inside her, even if she didn't know it at the time. Can you do something you fear, even if you're not able to see the consequences clearly?

_____

_____

_____

_____

The Sorceress and the Angels

Rev. Nina Roe

*W*ithin me resides a powerful sorceress…and a big, fat liar. It's okay, though, because the lies I speak of aren't the ones that made Pinocchio's nose grow. Rather, they're the subconscious scripts running endlessly beneath the surface of my thought, which pull me away from the foundation of who I am. They are the lies we all tell ourselves in order to make the truth go away.

So who am I, truly? The sorceress, or the liar? The heavens set me up to ask this question from the start. It took six weeks for my parents to name me. Make no mistake: this had nothing to do with neglect. My parents have adored me since conception. But I was the last child, and the only girl, and all those delicious names they'd been saving up had to be diplomatically sorted and assigned. Still, this is fascinating to me. How can you have a baby in the house with no name? What do you call her? "The baby?" "Her?" "She who's crying over there?" I wish I could have been a fly on the wall to observe.

The first six years of my life were a happy, blissful time. A highly sensitive child, I lived in a realm predominated by truth, surrounded by a family who allowed me to express myself in an almost unlimited number of creative ways. My sorceress was free to draw upon all her powers because I felt safe and cherished, with permission to be me. When I entered first grade, however, my delicate energy took its first real hit. Suddenly, I was forced to comply with a world that seemed harsh and, frankly, ridiculous at times. For purposes of self-preservation, I began to pretend I was someone I wasn't. In other words, I lied to fit in. With each deceitful thought that I wasn't already perfect, my sorceress wilted and withered.

21

One sunny day, our gym teacher was organizing a game of kickball. I was mortified at the possibility that I might be chosen last. Even though I was one of the taller, more athletic girls, I was also one of the more obnoxious and awkward ones. There was posturing to be done before that pivotal moment of team selection, and I worked my angle frantically. "Pick me, pick me!" I pleaded with one of the team captains. "Don't you want me on your team? Because I think you're just, just…Just the *best*, most popular girl here. I will do *anything* if you'll pick me first."

I lied. Ouch. It hurts just remembering that.

Flash forward to high school. Same all-girl private institution, different building. I'd just finished dating the second of three Peters in my life. The breakup hadn't been my choice, and I was devastated. I had evolved beyond my awkward, obnoxious younger self, and was popular now—but only barely. My tenuous hold on public approval drove me to date my ex's best friend. I couldn't be labeled "single"—and what better way to say "I am *so* over you" than to couple with the frenemy? The whole relationship was a lie. Every kiss made me cringe, and the prom was a nightmare. (My sincere apologies, J!) At the time, I only had eyes for Peter the Second. Double ouch.

Admittedly, these are small things, immature choices made by an unstable young girl. But since then, I've learned to ask myself, "If I'm lying about these small things, what's happening with the bigger ones?" Early in life, I lied to create situations which I thought were easier or better—but what was happening years down the road, with life-defining decisions like, "Is this job what my soul is meant to be doing?" Or, "Am I raising my children to be happy, or only to be successful by society's standards?" Were my subconscious, habitual lies keeping me bound to a life of limitation—and *imitation*—that didn't always feel good or authentic?

As an adult, I think the biggest lie I told myself was that I needed to live up to my generation's motto: "I am woman, hear me roar! I can work full-time as a successful corporate executive *and* be a loving, available mother *and* be a loving, available wife, *and* still be sane."

Yeah, right. Should I leap tall buildings in a single bound, too?

In my late thirties, I realized just how big a lie this was for me, and released my expectations. Perhaps it was a tiny step for women everywhere, but it was definitely a giant step toward the truth for this baby boomer. With my decision, the tide turned, and the little liar in me began to retreat, giving way to the power of my inner sorceress. Despite the terrifying prospect of cutting our income by more than half and risking isolation, the voice inside who knew better told me things were going to be just fine—perfect, even.

As I listened more and more closely, I began to see that people were looking to me for spiritual direction and guidance. I had taken an angel communication class with Doreen Virtue for fun, and one day, while I was in the pet store I used to own, a woman asked me to teach her how to read angel cards. Somewhat reluctantly, I agreed—and suddenly, I had a class of seven inspired women! My sorceress was leading me (with baby steps) toward the realization that I am here to teach the world that Angels are aspects of the higher Self, and that their wings represent the path of freedom.

If my inner sorceress had shown me this path ten years prior, I would have had myself committed. But she knows exactly what I can handle. She is my grounded vehicle for pulling all the goodness in my life together. She has the capacity to follow guidance from the Angels, listen to the wisdom of ascended masters, draw truth from friends and neighbors, and combine all this with a dollop of human ego and the reality of life in this body in order to create a magical, empowered existence. This doesn't mean that my little liar doesn't whisper things like, "You can't do this!" or "What will people think?" But I hear from her less and less these days. When I do, I say, "Well, hello there, little liar! I honor the fact that you've brought me to where I am today, but it's time for you to go. The sorceress is in command now."

Recently, I was fired by my dentist. I liked her well enough, but she wasn't happy about my decision to refuse X-rays, even with a signed waiver. You see, I've developed a rule: I only allow X-rays every two to three years, if a situation arises indicating a real need, or if my sorceress says "do it." I don't get X-rays simply because it's routine in the dental world, because when I take authority away from my sorceress, I take it away from *me*. In the past, my little liar would have denied my inner sense of knowing, and as a result would have exposed my body (and my pocketbook) to a procedure I knew was unnecessary. It seems like a small thing, but it still would have been a lie.

The Bible says, "And you will know the truth, and the truth will make you free." (John 8:32) But how can the truth make me free? How does it bring me closer to realizing the divine abilities of my inner sorceress, whom I know to be a woman capable of creating anything from the Divine Source of All That Is?

The fact is, we lie all the time. I've lied to protect loved ones from something I believed would disturb them. I've lied to protect myself from the backlash of another person's pain. I've lied out of habit, and because it's faster, easier, and simpler than telling the truth. I've lied because I'm scared of what the truth could reveal about me.

Several years ago, the Angels worked through my son to help me with this awakening. I was reprimanding him for lying about something—I can't even remember what. His response: "Mom, everyone lies."

Now, I would expect such a response from my bright, defiant, Indigo daughter, but never from my complacent, easygoing boy. I was shocked.

"I don't lie!" I insisted.

"Sure, you do," he said. "Think about it."

So I did. And I have, ever since.

Reflecting on more than four decades as a sensitive female in an often harsh world, I've come to understand that my journey of authenticity is based on answering just one question: "Who am I, really?" Each time I ask it, I answer with the truth as I know it: "I am one with the Divine Source of the Universe. I am a powerful sorceress." Every miscalculation, script, or belief that runs counter to this truth is a lie that whittles away at my God-given strength and undermines my mission. Becoming my authentic self has involved looking this fact straight in the eye. I've learned to be aware when the little liar inside surfaces, and reassure her that it's okay to trust in the truth, to speak it and be it. In this way, the truth has indeed set me free.

I still avoid wearing my school colors, but my dentist has taken me back on my terms, and I continue to evolve by embracing the truth that I am a powerful Sorceress—as are we all.

And so it is!

TUNE IN TO YOUR *Authentic* SELF

As Nina's son pointed out to her, "Everyone lies." What do you lie about? What do you omit?

_____

_____

_____

_____

Have you ever felt that a lie undermined your inner power—your "sorceress?" Why did you tell that lie, and what were the results?

_____

_____

_____

_____

What do you think would happen if you stopped lying for a day, even to protect your loved ones or smooth things over at work? How might speaking your truth enable you to live more authentically?

_____

_____

_____

_____

CHAPTER TWO

PASSING THROUGH THE *Valley*

Invisible to Irresistible

Christine Laureano

S omeone once said to me, "What would you know about feeling bad? You look like you have a perfect life!"

Well, maybe I do look all put-together in my 5'9" blond frame. But when it comes to the forks in the road, where the bigger lessons present themselves, we all have choices to make: go right, or go left.

I was always different, especially when it came to my thoughts and ideas. As a kid, I struggled to fit in. I understood things that other kids my age couldn't grasp. At eleven, I understood the story of Jonathan Livingston Seagull as a parable to moving through planes of consciousness. At thirteen, I felt the conflict around understanding the outside world and the illusion behind it as experienced by the main character in Plato's *The Cave*. I resonated with the teachings of Ghandi, Mother Theresa, and the Dalai Lama. When I read Dale Carnegie's *How to Win Friends and Influence People*, I knew I wanted to do something that would help people feel good about themselves— their authentic selves.

There were some adults with whom I could talk about my ideas, my mother being one of them. But I still felt like I didn't belong, and that was painful. When I was with my peers, I felt a shift happening.

I reached the first fork in the road in middle school. The new ice rink in town had just been finished, and one afternoon my friends and I went skating. I glided out onto the wonderful, smooth surface of the ice, and whipped around the rink, fully expecting everyone else to be right beside me. But when I looked back, I saw that they were just

29

getting their "ice legs," wobbling along the wall, holding on to each other for support.

I felt their stares and heard their whispers. I was shining and standing out—not fitting in. So what did I do?

I took the wrong fork in the path. And I fell from grace, right onto my ass.

From that point on, the light inside me began to dim. I went back to the edge of the rink, and only showed some of the "real" me—the me who didn't make other people uncomfortable.

I kept finding the right forks and then choosing the wrong forks until I was thirty-two, when I had my first child, Alexa. With her, I felt a connection like no other. I was her mom, and she was my little angel. On the day she was born, I looked into her deep brown, beautiful eyes, and I could see the old soul inside her, wise beyond words.

Alexa's death in day care, just four months and twenty-two days after she entered my world, was the most profoundly awful lesson life had ever offered me. Everything was ripped out from under me. The fork in the path met the dark canyon, and it brought me to my knees.

I spent a month on the couch, feeling beyond sad, and more lonely than I'd ever felt in my life. I was completely empty, alone in the canyon of despair. And then one day it came to me: what would Dale Carnegie suggest?

I got off the couch, showered (finally) and drove to the bookstore. I needed to be around people without actually engaging with anyone, in a place where no one knew me. I couldn't endure the awkward looks of people who knew there was nothing they could say to make it better.

In dire need of reconnection, I went to the self-help section, though I doubted there was anything there that could help me. At first, the titles all just ran together. But then, a book on angels by Silver Ravenwolf literally jumped out at me. I hadn't connected to my spiritual side for a long time; I'd let that place go in order to fit in, all those years ago. But that day, as I held that book in my hands, the gates opened, and I was flooded with an awareness that had been buried deep inside of me. I realized that I was thirsting for answers. *Why* had this happened to my daughter? *Why* had this happened to me and my family? *Why* did it have to be her and not me? *Why* was I here when she wasn't?

My soul already had the answers, but the books were the catalyst that helped to bring my inner wisdom to the surface. I understood at last why Alexa had come, and why she left. The messages and feelings I received were deep and real. "Touch the lives of people who are in your shoes," my inner voice said. "Be vulnerable so you can help others heal." In order to teach people the importance of listening to the soul's calling, I had to become real and genuine.

Although I was still scared of shining in a big way, I took the first steps toward my calling. I received certification as a life coach, and I became the teacher. The on-again, off-again connection I'd had with myself during the years before Alexa's birth shaped the three-step process I use in my business today to help people spiral up, discover their unique gifts and talents, and shine in their authenticity.

31

My process emerged as a natural progression of the divine life lessons I experienced. It begins with *awareness*, the opening of our conscious mind to the potential and possibilities within our souls. Next, we *elevate*, making decisions that enable us to move forward toward our dreams and intentions. And finally, we *achieve* by manifesting our intentions and living true to our purpose.

My process was working, and I knew that what I was teaching helped people. But in 2010, I fell into invisibility again. I reached another fork in the path, and tumbled headfirst into a subtle and drawn-out lesson.

I'd proclaimed that 2010 was going to be the year of monumental growth in my business. I was ready to hear clients pounding down my door, and see my name in lights. I learned how to build my contact list, created e-mail campaigns, and did all the "right" things to set myself up for a golden year.

But instead of feeling empowered, I was frustrated. I felt the spin of confusion inside of me, like I'd been riding the Tilt-a-Whirl at the carnival. And the "success" I was experiencing was nowhere near the goals I'd set for myself.

What I realized after ten long months was that, once again, I'd been playing by someone else's rules. I had followed other people's models, and ended up losing my authenticity in the name of marketing. What I was offering didn't really represent my quirky, unique, "real" self. Instead of relying on the advice of business gurus, I needed to listen to my intuition.

Awareness is the first step to which I bring my clients, but it literally took a breakdown to bring me out of my own abyss. My husband tells me I'm as deep as an angler fish—you know, the fish that, by its own glowing stalk, illuminates its way through the abyss of the unknown. I am no stranger to the deeper work, but by trying, once again, to fit in with "them," I'd stopped shining my light.

Once more, I asked myself the tough questions. Who am I being? What do I want? Are the visions and goals I've created really mine, or are they someone else's? Why am I here? And once again, the answers were right there in plain sight, just waiting for my inner light—my authentic awareness—to illuminate them.

This time, the climb out of the canyon wasn't anywhere near as hard. I just had to get back to being me. The lessons I'd learned from Alexa once again came to the forefront. The tipping point was when I saw the cover of a popular magazine. The headlines on that issue read,

"Own Your Power! Unlock Your Inner Superstar! Let Your Best Self Shine!"—right alongside those perfect fall shoes. The Universe was splashing its message to me all over the front cover. How could I teach others to be authentic when I wasn't walking my talk? I didn't want to market to people: I wanted to *move* them!

Today, I believe that Alexa's life ended so mine could come back. I miss her presence every day—but her departure brought me to my most authentic self. She is the reason I put my proverbial skates back on, and why I feel great about shining. And when I come to another fork in the road, I trust that the Universe, and Alexa's beautiful spirit, will surely illuminate the direction I need to take.

TUNE IN TO YOUR *Authentic* SELF

Have you ever suppressed your authentic self in order to fit in with others? What frightened you about letting your light shine?

_____

_____

_____

_____

When we're scared to shine, it's often because we don't want to get hurt—but sometimes, being authentic also means being vulnerable. What are your feelings about vulnerability, and how might they be helping or hindering you on your authentic path?

_____

_____

_____

_____

Do you take advice from those you admire, even when their methods don't feel authentic to you? What would it look like if you trusted yourself and acted on your instincts, rather than following the "established" road?

_____

_____

_____

_____

Message from an Angel

Sharon Babineau

"**M**ommy."

I turned toward my daughter, following the soft trail of her voice.

"Please promise me that you will be happy."

Her words hung in the air. Their meaning took my breath away. Under any other circumstances her request might have seemed simple; attainable, even. But not now. Not like this.

My beautiful daughter Maddie had just relapsed for the third time, and despite her courageous determination and all the difficult treatments she'd endured, the cancer continued to ravage her body. A cure was no longer deemed possible.

I was devastated, and spent all my time focusing solely on her. I had retreated from the world. And here she was, looking to comfort me.

She smiled gently. "Promise me you will be happy after I'm gone." As if she was afraid for me, and of how I would react.

The words hit me hard. I felt sick. The room began to spin. I fought hard to stay calm. I wanted to run. I had prayed that we would never have this painful conversation, but now the ugly truth of our situation, the dreadful reality of it, was finally out in the open.

Maddie had been battling bone cancer since the tender age of twelve. She was heroic in her fight, but it spread, again and again. Incredibly, she used her precious energy to make sure everyone she loved—everyone she was leaving behind—would be okay.

"Mommy," she said, "I'm not afraid to die. I am more worried for you and Derek. So don't be sad. Be happy. Do it for me, and for my brother. He deserves to be happy too."

I wished that I could be anywhere but there, at that threshold where life dies and death lives. Such a fine line; we were crossing over to the unknown, and my worst nightmare was coming true. I had been holding on to the faint hope that she would beat her cancer, like she had twice before. She was only fifteen years old; she had only begun to live her life. It wasn't fair.

I wished I could scoop her up in my arms, like I had when she was a young child with a skinned knee. I wished I could hug her and tell her that everything would be okay, that there must be a mistake, and that I would fix everything, because that's what mommies are for. But I couldn't hide from this. There was nothing I could do, no bandage I could put over this wound. The only thing I could do was to stand strong and be as brave as she was. I had to face the truth. My beautiful daughter was dying.

"I promise, Maddie," I told her. "I will try to be happy."

On May 15, 2007, shortly after that heartbreaking conversation, Maddie earned her wings to heaven.

I will never forget her final message. Hers were true words of wisdom: courageous, spoken from a place of deep love. At the time, though, I refused to see the good in them. I didn't understand the power they held. I thought the promise I made to her—to be happy—was a burden, a curse. I made the promise, but I didn't believe I could ever keep it. How could anyone be happy after they had buried a child? She had asked the impossible!

I spiraled into despair. I thought about how unfair life could be. A few years before Maddie became sick, my husband Stephen died of ALS (Lou Gehrig's disease) after a nine year battle. There was nothing I could do to save him. When Maddie was diagnosed, I vowed to do everything in my power to keep her alive—and yet, I couldn't.

I tried to be happy, for my son Derek's sake. He deserved to be happy, and to have a mom who was happy. But the truth was that I was just going through the motions. I looked normal on the outside, but felt very broken on the inside.

Throughout my life, I had always been a happy-go-lucky person. Sure, there had been difficult times, but I was always able to see the silver lining. I prided myself on being an optimist—but not anymore. After I lost my daughter, I no longer believed I deserved to be happy. My family of four had become two, and the world seemed bigger, colder, and scarier. I started to see everything differently. No longer carefree, I was afraid, full of doubt and anger. I withdrew from life.

37

Searching for support, I started to correspond with a woman who had also lost a daughter, and to the same disease. She shared with me that she was still in the same amount of pain as she had been when her daughter passed away.

"How long has it been," I asked her.

"Twenty-three years," she replied.

In twenty-three years, she hadn't been able to move forward at all with her life. As she continued to share her story, it seemed to me that she wore her grief on her sleeve; it consumed her.

It pained me to imagine a life so full of agony. I couldn't believe her daughter would have wanted her to linger in an unhappy existence. It was as if two people had died that day, more than two decades ago: the daughter, and the mother, whose sadness prevented her from living a purposeful life.

Then, it hit me. I remembered Maddie's words. My daughter had generously given me permission to be happy. I finally realized that the promise I made that day was a blessing; a gift, not a burden. How wise my daughter was! How lucky I was to have received her gift!

Now that I finally understood the meaning of her message, I made a conscious choice to fulfill my promise: to be happy, and to find gratitude daily in my life. Yes, my life had changed. Yes, my trust was shaken. But there was still hope for the future.

It wasn't easy to rebuild my life without Maddie and Stephen, but I committed myself to making the best of it—not only for Derek, but for me. "What better way to honor my husband and daughter," I thought, "than to live my life fully?"

The old saying, "Fake it 'til you make it," helps for a while, but the heart knows the difference. My heart had been broken; it felt like there was a black, bottomless hole in it. So I went within. I couldn't heal my life unless I healed my heart first.

Every day, I would wake up and meditate on gratitude. This became my ritual. Each morning, I found something, anything, to be grateful for. I was so very grateful for my son—but I also became grateful for simple things, like the weather, food, and friends. Things I had once taken for granted, I learned to embrace in the present. I chose my thoughts carefully, and questioned the negative ones.

As I found gratitude, the pain lessened. I felt more in control, less a victim of circumstance. I learned to celebrate the wonderful moments I had shared with Stephen and Maddison. Our journey together, considered too short in Earth years, was eternal in my heart. I celebrated what I had learned as the mother of a child with cancer, because I had been granted a rare glimpse into a truly heroic journey.

I learned that happiness is a choice—but more than that, I realized that I truly wanted to be happy. I *needed* to be happy. Happiness is part of my essence. It is who I am.

Slowly, food began to taste good again. Passion came back into my life. I became active; exercising, running, and playing hockey. I found purpose in volunteer work, and enjoyed time with my son. After more than ten years as a widow, I opened my heart to love, and recently remarried. I felt my daughter with me on that special day; her love and wisdom filled my heart.

I know that if I hadn't *chosen* to be happy, I would never have returned to my authentic self. Now, I see the world in all its glory, and look to the future with renewed energy and excitement. I feel whole again.

I embrace my passion for helping others, and empower them to embrace their own right to happiness, because happiness is an "inside job." I feel as if I have a secret to share—a secret passed to me by my angel, Maddie—and I share it through books, keynotes, workshops, and retreats.

May my secret guide you to be happy, too.

TUNE IN TO YOUR *Authentic* SELF

Are you happy? What does happiness mean to you?

_____

_____

_____

_____

What events in your past, or what current circumstances, do you feel "prevent" you from experiencing happiness?

_____

_____

_____

_____

Sharon writes that the woman with whom she connected "wore her grief on her sleeve; it consumed her," even twenty-three years later. Traumatic events are hard to process, but when our reactions to events or circumstances become our identity, they draw us away from our authenticity. Is your identification with grief or loss preventing you from living fully in the now? How can you shift this while still honoring your experience?

_____

_____

_____

_____

Inside Out

Aimée Yawnick

"Living an amazing life doesn't come by trying to be amazing, but rather by recognizing the amazing that is already within you and allowing that beauty to emerge."
- Marsh Engle

I was twenty-one the first time I was engaged. Of course I accepted. It was a no-brainer, a win-win situation. I was able to avoid my fear (okay, terror) of being alone. Plus it was the ultimate act of defiance, guaranteed to annoy my mother like nothing else I could do.

Round two came at age twenty-eight. This fellow had a different name and a different face, but on the inside he was just more of the same. This time wasn't as much fun (since my mom was still mad at me from round one), but it still warranted another "yes."

41

Now, I recognize that it was my strong inner wisdom that made sure I called off both engagements before the fateful "I do" ceremonies. Now, when I recall the moments around both proposals, I can hear the little voice inside me saying, "You'll never marry this guy. There's something better out there for you." At the time, though, I ignored the voice, and said "yes" anyway, because being in a loveless relationship where I was controlled, emotionally abused, and kept under lock and key not only felt oddly familiar, it was less scary than being alone.

Up to that point, in my dealings with men, I had never experienced feeling valued, adored, loved, or respected. I had no idea how to look for such things, let alone how to ask for them—so I just kept attracting men who gave me what I knew, and what I was expecting.

When I was thirty-three, something amazing happened: my world fell apart. The career that I'd loved for almost ten years ended. I walked away from my fiancé, my house, and my dog (the most heart-wrenching goodbye of the three!) and found myself heading home to Mom with my tail between my legs. After I'd so cruelly battered her feelings when I hooked up with Loser #2, knocking on her door was the ultimate exercise in humility.

I was jobless, and for the first time in my adult life, manless. It was the best thing that ever happened to me.

That falling apart was the start of my journey inward. I began with traditional therapy, and eventually found my calling in coaching. (There were many bumps along the way, and it isn't a path that ever ends, but more on that later.)

Given my dismal track record, I decided the wisest plan was to swear off men forever. Eventually, though, I ditched that idea for "Plan B," and decided to take another chance on love and open myself to the possibility of a new romance. You know what they say: "Third time's the charm!" Or is it "Three strikes and you're out?" Anyway, I did what I said I'd never do and joined an online dating service. In less than three months, I met Prince Charming! He swept me away on his big white steed, and we are now living happily ever after.

Well, maybe it didn't happen exactly that way.

Although I had done a lot of work on myself, I had no idea how to "be" in a relationship with a man—at least, not in a *healthy* relationship. What I knew for sure was that I was not going to let history repeat itself. This time I was going to do it right. Something had to change, and that something was me.

I remember very clearly the moment when I had to choose between my old ways and something new. My boyfriend, Adam, was adamant about communication. (Imagine that!) He insisted, in a very kind and loving way, that we talk, often, about our feelings.

"Who is this guy?" I wondered. "What planet is he from?" Meaningful conversations with a boyfriend were completely foreign to me.

One day, as I waited for Adam to come home from work, I suddenly knew that if I wasn't willing to share and give of myself, be vulnerable, and express my real feelings, I would certainly lose this man. I started to sob.

I shared this realization with Adam and, being the honest and genuine man he is, he confirmed my fears. He wouldn't want to stay in a relationship in which he was denied knowing the real me.

That was when I made the decision to *be* my authentic self; now, I just had to *find* her! I had no idea who the real Aimée was, but I knew that I could, and must, express to Adam whatever was going on inside me.

43

What a blessing! Talking about my search allowed me to identify more and more pieces of the elusive, authentic me. These were my defining moments. I was repeatedly challenged to stretch out of my comfort zone, express my feelings, and share my dreams and fears, all in the name of love and the vulnerability that comes with it. I soon learned that the vulnerable Aimée is who I am at my best; my real, authentic self. It's also the scariest place on earth for me. I can only describe it as turning myself inside out.

It wasn't uncommon for me to hear that I was unapproachable; that I always looked angry, and that it was difficult to get to know me. I had built up a tough outer shell to make sure I couldn't be hurt, and so that the people around me couldn't discover some horrible part of me that would cause them to leave forever.

I had many acquaintances, but very few close friends. I was a great listener, but never shared of myself. I was fun at parties, but afterwards I went home alone, closed the door, and shut off the phone. Don't call me, I'll call you.

Don't you just love how the Universe provides exactly what you need, when you need it? On the heels of my new willingness to open up, I began my coach training, as well as a rigorous curriculum of personal development courses. Talk about trial by fire! There were more than enough chances to open myself up to others and be vulnerable, and I discovered that it does, in fact, get easier with practice.

Once I warmed up to the process of turning myself inside out, I discovered that my hard exterior shell hid a warm, fuzzy center. I shared this newfound fuzziness with Adam, and guess what? He didn't run away! He didn't reject me when I revealed my ugly warts, or judge me when I shared my darkest secrets. As long as I was being the real, authentic me—transparent, tender and vulnerable—he gave me all kinds of positive reinforcement. He would say, "Thank you for sharing a part of yourself with me." Then, he would ask to learn more.

Adam may not have swept me away on his big white steed, but he did rescue me in many ways, and we *are* living happily ever after. At the time of this writing, we have been together for eight years, and will celebrate our third wedding anniversary next month. I guess "they" were right after all: the third time is the charm! After two failed engagements I had come to accept that perhaps marriage wasn't in the cards for me. This is just one more way that my relationship with Adam is a miracle for me; a whole new ball game. For the first time in my life, the man I love also loves and accepts me. Good and bad, he loves everything. And guess what? So do I!

Since I turned myself inside out, I have been grateful for every moment. When I am being my authentic self, I shine. My heart opens up. I connect with my Divine purpose, and am free to just be me, however that may look in that moment. I won't lie to you: it took a lot of work to get to this place. I make a conscious decision every day to be the woman I really am. Every time I make that choice, though, I create depth in a relationship, connect with another human being on a more meaningful level, and feel my connection to God grow stronger.

When I help another person see themselves through my eyes—and as God sees them—I am every bit my authentic self. This is who I am for my clients. Every one of us has a place deep in our core where we are so tender and vulnerable that the mere thought of anyone else seeing it sends us running for the hills. But this is the place where authenticity lives: our common humanity, our Divine purpose for being alive, and our ability to lead a life that touches and elevates the lives of others.

So turn yourself inside out, and let your authentic light shine!

TUNE IN TO YOUR *Authentic* SELF

When her world "fell apart," Aimée recognized that she'd unconsciously been making bad relationship choices out of fear. Do you choose your relationships consciously or unconsciously?

_____

_____

_____

_____

How can you bring elements of your true, vulnerable nature to light in your everyday life?

_____

_____

_____

_____

When we allow ourselves to be vulnerable, we also allow ourselves to be compassionate to others—to see them, as Aimée writes, "as God sees them." How can you harness the power of your own vulnerability to connect with your loved ones on a deeper level?

CHAPTER THREE

_____

_____

_____

_____

SPIRITUAL
Awakening

Grandmothers' Circle

Kari Henley

I was the kind of kid who wondered about God at an early age. I asked to go to church, but didn't find what I was looking for—and talked to the stars instead. I would escape to a nearby park and ask for help from a grove of huge, swaying trees. They felt like giant grandmothers to me; wise, gnarled, yet full of levity. Their leaves, shimmering in the breeze, always whispered the answers I needed.

Later, I studied traditional religions, New Age fads, and Jungian psychology. I have great appreciation for the many ways we seek communion with Source. Some pray to Mary, Jesus, Shiva, the Great Creator, or angels. For me, my innocent talks with the grandmother trees evolved into an unusual etheric connection with an elder counsel which informed my spiritual life. When I was twenty-four, I received a vision of a circle of wise grandmothers sitting in a tipi, and have had movie-style teachings ever since.

49

"The grandmothers" have remained a very private part of my life—it's not very normal, after all! When I need them, or hear them call, the ritual to begin is consistently specific. I close my eyes and see myself standing on top of a rocky cliff similar to the Grand Canyon. A guide comes for me, and together we fly into a hidden box canyon where the grandmothers' grand tipi awaits.

When I arrive, I must prepare by a fire. When at last I enter the tent, I spontaneously smile. The grandmothers are irreverent, serious, funny, and intense all at once. Their presence is a visceral warmth; it emanates from the wrinkled softness of their leathery skin, gnarled fingers, and sparkling eyes. Usually when I visit I am distraught about something, and they offer matter of fact, no-bullshit advice I wouldn't have considered on my own. My invited meditations with them are like being in confessional at a church, or praying in a temple. It is communion.

I have made this journey off and on for twenty years. My apprenticeship with the grandmothers reminds me how to live an authentic life. They push me, comfort me, and make me laugh with their cackling jokes. When teaching women's retreats, I have led guided visualizations to connect women with their own circle of ancient wise women. So many women eagerly relate to the comfort of finding their own ancient feminine lineage, an element sadly missing in our culture today. Grandmother wisdom is universal, and touches a place of deep recognition.

One of my most powerful miracles came when I was thirty-one, and newly pregnant with my second child. I was in an unhappy marriage, and the stress caused me to start to miscarry. Suddenly, I felt the grandmothers whisper, "Lie on the couch." Scared, yet trusting, I closed my eyes. I could see the grandmothers all around me, chanting, hovering their hands over my womb. One ancient face floated directly into mine; she said that she held the spirit of my unborn daughter, and would give me strength. I stopped bleeding immediately.

During that pregnancy, I felt the grandmothers almost constantly, as I drew the courage to leave my marriage with my toddler son in tow. I had just been laid off from my job, was far away from my family, and felt totally alone—but somehow I knew if I did not leave while my baby was still tucked inside, I never would.

My therapist introduced me to two women who needed a place to live for a year: one with a son the same age as my toddler, and the other a fantastic midwife just returning from Central America to start her practice. I was pampered and held. I believe the grandmothers guided me to the right people to transform my life.

We found a beautiful oceanside home we could afford, and I discovered the magic of living in a sweet communal space of women. One of my deepest dreams was to have a home birth, and I knew the coincidence was divine guidance. With my doctor's blessing, I made another leap. The night I went into labor, instead of rushing to a hospital, I simply went upstairs, where my midwife roommate lit candles, played native music, and in three hours brought my "little grandmother" gently into the world.

The grandmothers were fairly quiet after that. Years later, I'd remarried, had twins, and was raising our family while writing for the Huffington Post and leading virtual events. One day, after hosting a tele-summit of fifty-seven calls in thirty-one days, interviewing one hundred women luminaries from all over the world, I decided to treat myself to a well-deserved massage. I had never felt so honored, so alive—or so exhausted.

I knew I was ripe for another quantum leap in my life, yet residual fears gnawed at my edges. Could I really manage a career and four kids? Was I truly worthy? My daughter was now twelve, and had started suffering from intense anxiety attacks that brought me to my knees. I needed a break. Lying on the massage table, I slipped between the sheets, put my head in the cradle and sighed.

No sooner had I closed my eyes than I felt a familiar pull. The grandmothers were calling me.

I felt to the core of my being that this was serious, and allowed my mind to obediently drift. The vision began at the grandmothers' grand tipi. They briskly informed me I had to come the "old way," back to the cliff, but this time I had to find my way to the box canyon alone.

"Oh my God," I gulped. This was initiation. It was time to fly.

A marvelous dance commenced. As the massage therapist's hands worked specific parts of my body, it triggered guided insights I never could have made alone. As she started rubbing my body, I was standing alone at the cliff, as I always did when I came here—but this time, I wore a beautiful cream-and-gold gown. I looked over the edge; the pull of the precipice jolted me to the core. I am terrified of heights, and my stomach lurched. I took a deep breath. I could do this.

The grandmothers' raspy voices crooned in my ear. As my arms were being massaged, they began their lesson. "In order to fly, you must build strength in your arms. When you leap, flap like crazy to get some lift. Once you get going, you can relax—and soar." I took in the power of this lesson as my arms were gently replaced under the blankets. Next, I heard the slather of more oil, and warm hands moved to my neck and back.

"There is no looking behind when you are flying, or you will dip and move off course. Focus ahead, toward the sun," they continued. "When looking to the past, full flight is impossible. Stay in the moment, concentrate on what is ahead, and let everything slip away with the passing clouds."

As the aches in my back were released by expert fingers, the inner voices kept speaking. "Soaring above the crowd requires a backbone. Release the weight on your shoulders. You don't need it anymore." With a final swish of oil, my legs were stroked and I was reminded, "Sometimes it is easier to stay in the clouds instead of facing reality. Land on the Earth with strong legs, and walk with pride."

The initiation was complete. When I arrived, the fire was already lit. I entered the grandmothers' tent, and saw an open seat waiting for me. Through years of following my intuition and growing gray hair, I had earned my place. "Welcome sister," they said. We grabbed hands and closed our eyes. Their faces were young and ancient all at once, just like I knew my own would be.

As I continue to walk my personal path, authenticity for me now means being a teacher, rather than a student. The grandmothers give me courage to make the choices that lead my path toward its inevitable conclusion: sharing, rather than simply accumulating, wisdom. I am grateful for their lifelong tutelage.

As I came back to myself on the massage table, I knew. Outside the tent, and far away at the edge of the precipice, the next apprentice was waiting. It was my daughter, and I was ready for her.

TUNE IN TO YOUR
Authentic SELF

Have you ever received a message from a spiritual "advisor?"

_____

_____

_____

_____

Kari's near-miscarriage brought her closer to the grandmothers, but in order for them to help, she had to trust the process. What would happen if you were to put your faith and fear in the hands of Source or your spiritual guides?

54

_____

_____

_____

_____

Often in order to progress to the next part of our path, we are asked to do the things we think we cannot do. Kari was asked to fly, despite her fear of heights, and came through to a brand new phase of her authentic life. What fears and roadblocks stand in your way right now? How can you embrace the lessons they teach you?

_____

_____

_____

_____

Cosmic Timeout

Andra Evans

“*T*his morning, in a sleepy waking dream, Buffalo came to me, walking toward me first as a luminous outline, revealing her wise eyes, dewy nose, and glistening horns through a misty morning fog. As she moved closer, she "solidified" into a more tangible furry being...I could hear her breathing as we stood face to face, in unconditional acceptance of each other, as if her appearance into my awareness was a destined meeting. I felt grace and reverence for her visit, and wondered what her message was. There was peace and wisdom in her eyes, and with a childlike wonder, feeling this visit was a good omen, I smiled softly as a wave of bliss rushed through my body. I radiated love and telepathically thanked her for coming, and with a snort and light shake of her expansive head and furry mane, she dissolved back into the mist.*”

- Journal entry, May 18, 2011

55

This is a story of being called to my true path—a story of awakening from a life clouded by a limited perspective to the path I walk today, embracing the love and abundance of a universe filled with purpose, creativity, and magic.

I went through most of my life not believing in a higher power, god, or source. The way I was brought up left me suspicious and cynical about the world of religion. I preferred to think of "the meaning of life" as something personal to be discovered. By mid-life, I was in search of my spiritual identity, and I was in for a bumpy wake-up call.

As soon as I turned forty, it was as if my life flashed before me for review. Something stirred within me that told me change was in the wind. I had a decent job and a good group of friends, and was a single, fun-loving homeowner in Vancouver. But I also had a history of mild depression, which had kept a cloud hanging over me for almost two decades. In my twenties, I was prescribed antidepressants to manage stress; now, at forty, I was still on them, wondering if they were contributing to me feeling just okay about my life, versus loving it.

It was this which sparked my passion for spirituality and consciousness, and led me to seek out natural treatments for depression that looked at the body-mind-spirit connection. Under the supervision of my doctor, I weaned myself off of the antidepressants, and began taking vitamins, minerals, and herbs. I also changed my diet and focused on my yoga and meditation practice. Thanks to these shifts, along with my spiritual studies, I started opening to new worlds of awareness. I started experiencing random expanded states of consciousness—seeing, hearing, and feeling energy, and at times feeling bigger than my body. It was as if my brain was being rewired. It was amazing and inviting, and felt like pure love pouring down from the cosmos.

Was I "waking up," I wondered?

In 2006 I decided to leave my job, cash in my stock options, and go back to school to become a counselor. Counseling felt like my true calling: my education was in psychology and communications, and I envisioned a career focused on helping people manage change, develop spiritual understanding, and step toward their true selves.

I enrolled in a program, but it ended up not being quite the right fit. The morning I was supposed to start my second term, something weird happened. I was just about to get out of bed when I felt something gently hold me down. I heard a whisper say, "*Just stop.*" I lay there, not moving, wondering what was happening. I felt like I was not alone. Then, I heard the words, *"Do not go back."*

My intuition was telling me that I was at the wrong school. Despite what was at stake, despite the fact that I had changed my whole life to follow a new path, I felt the truth of those words and surrendered. I didn't go back.

Instead, I turned my focus inward. But I had no job, no school, no partner, and no clue what to do next except bawl my heart out and ask for help. I felt like I had sabotaged myself, and the hole I'd dug was too deep to get out of.

In my despair, I began calling out to something I had never believed in before—that presence which had told me to "stop." Over the span of about a week, I began hearing more whispers. *"Be still." "Listen." "Go outside." "Get ready." "You are not who you think you are."*

I continued my spiritual studies, began healing my ego and soul, did shadow work, and learned about co-creative manifesting. I went for daily hikes, meditated, journaled, and practiced yoga. I opened to allowing spirit to be a presence in my life; this fed my dream world with animal spirit guides, who told me to retreat and change the way I looked at my circumstances and the world around me. Life and its beauty were shown to me, and I embraced it.

During this time, I started feeling the pull of home and family back in Toronto, where I was born. My parents were aging, and my sister had just been diagnosed with cancer. Plus I still had to figure out a way to proceed with my calling. The last whisper of guidance I got in Vancouver was, *"Heal yourself so you can help others."* And so, by the end of 2008, my Vancouver chapter was closed and I was home.

As soon as I arrived, it felt like a red carpet unfolded to greet me. I had crossed a threshold of challenge and was moving into something new and fresh. I attended, and graduated from, the school I was *supposed* to go to, and began a healing process that helped me understand my life as an empath (a trait which also helped to explain my depression).

I started studying with new teachers who helped me resurrect my creativity through art, music, and dance. I called on *A Course in Miracles* to heal my mind and spirit, and realized that my lack of relationship with my creator had affected my entire life, keeping me separate from *real* love, *real* power, and *real* creativity. I also called on *Women Who Run with the Wolves* to help me better understand the mystery of being a woman—a free, intuitive, magical being who passes through phases of knowing herself as she matures, and who courageously moves through shadows to reclaim gifts of vision, creativity, and wisdom out of the dark. I became a phoenix, rising out of the ashes of one phase of life and into the next.

My fortieth birthday in 2004 marked the beginning of a period in my life I will forever refer to as my "cosmic timeout." I took a leap of faith to pursue my true calling which brought me first to a dark night of the soul, then to a quest to find my truth underneath layers of life experience. Subsequently, I awakened to a new knowing that the mysteries of life offer more in the way of creative possibility than I could ever have imagined. I learned that those whispers I heard are from my "higher self," and that visits from spirit animals like Buffalo can offer me guidance about reclaiming my power. Buffalo's message is about manifesting abundance through right action, gratitude and prayer—a timely message, as I reach out with this story and continue to build my practice as a spiritual healer, teacher, and mentor.

Today, my life continues to be an adventure of discovering and harnessing the potential right in front of me. I am visioning my path forward as a "spirit walker," someone who co-creates with spirit to carve her destiny. Thanks to that necessary period of surrender, letting go, acceptance, healing, forgiveness, and allowing, I was able to make room for my divine self to emerge. I've cultivated a wiser, healthier me, a woman who knows the importance of the journey inward, and of being free-spirited—two things our culture does not typically value (although I hope to help change that)!

My cosmic timeout was my midlife initiation—a bridge between my previous life, where I was searching for meaning without really knowing what life was all about, to a life of purpose and alignment. Now I assist others with their own transitions, awakenings, and adventures in self-creation by sharing my gifts as a channel for divine love that heals. I am who I came here to be: a magical, self-determined woman, living an authentic life surrounded by love, support, community, opportunity, and a Universe that keeps calling me to play.

TUNE IN TO YOUR
Authentic SELF

What does spiritual practice mean to you? Has spirituality been a major part of your life thus far?

_____

_____

_____

_____

Andra's life changed when a divine presence told her to "just stop." When was the last time you received an intuitive message? What advice did that message hold?

_____

_____

_____

_____

Sometimes, we set off on what feels like an authentic path, only to find that we've been following the wrong branch. Andra's choice to follow her divine instruction and leave her first school felt like a setback, but in fact led her to her true place and calling. When was the last time a setback turned into a divine gift for you? Were you able to let go and trust during the process, or was the "rightness" of things revealed to you only after the fact?

_____

_____

_____

_____

She Speaks to Me

Lisa Michaels

*I*n 1988, it began growing as a longing, a hunger, a craving. My heart, body, and soul ached for the voice of the Divine Feminine. Everywhere I turned, for as long as I could remember, all I heard was God as "He," but somehow I knew I had to have "She" to claim all of myself.

Just to be clear, it wasn't a rejection of the masculine I was seeking. It wasn't about *him*; rather, it was a full-on inclusion experience of the feminine for which I yearned. I was amazed when I first realized that the word *she* also contains *he*. *Woman* holds *man*, *God* is found in *Goddess*, and *priest* is in *priestess*—but not the other way around.

61

Slowly, I pieced together a path to the sacred feminine in my life. I devoured the few books I found on the subject, and soon, *She* started saving my life in a multitude of subtle and profound ways. She helped me to find my authentic life guidance internally, and stop my endless search for answers outside of myself.

I began making life changes based on what I felt inside. One of the first things I did was to stop celebrating any "holiday" to which I didn't feel a real connection. Instead, I wanted to honor the seasons of nature. I took up gardening, and realized that being in nature could connect me more fully to my own inner nature. The natural world is fundamentally a cyclic creative force, and so is the core essence of the feminine.

As my need and understanding grew, I searched for connection to others who were having a similar experience. I gathered the courage to ask several women I knew if they would like to come together as a group to celebrate the seasons. Over the course of a year, we learned together how to honor each point on the Wheel of the Year. I researched each power day, and then we created a simple ceremony to work with the energy of that day.

I noticed several important things through that process. The Wheel of the Year power days arrive every six weeks, so I had to be on top of preparing the next ceremony almost as soon as I finished the last. This meant I needed to be constantly enjoying the present moment as well as releasing what had just happened and planning for what was coming next—just like in life! Most importantly, I gained a body-knowing about the cycles of change, and how the Wheel of the Year could help me work with all the layers of transformation once I understand its energies. As I connected to nature's rhythms, I started feeling more in sync with myself.

62 At the same time as I was working with the women's circle, I was also co-owner and director of a 500-pupil ballet school. I loved the formed shapes in ballet, but my body, newly attuned to nature and the Wheel of the Year, began urging me toward freer movement. I found that during an expressive, free type of dance, I could connect to my inner guidance and have profound insights. In the church of my childhood, dancing was considered a "sin," and throughout my life I had been searching for the full reconnection of my dancing and spirituality. This deepened as my free moving began.

I learned much later that the primary form of worship for the Goddess is dance. No wonder I loved it so much—and no wonder it was considered a "sin" by those whose motivation was to keep the feminine out of the sacred!

Much as I loved teaching ballet and running the school, my inner guidance eventually made it clear that it was time for the next step in my journey. When I left the school, I spent two years taking classes, diving deeply into a powerful and profound Goddess-based process, and reading everything I could get my hands on. Then, I started sharing my discoveries with others through a six-week class called "Awakening to the Divine Feminine."

Often I've felt that practicing my authentic feminine spirituality was like swimming upstream in a cultural river. Western spirituality is mostly dedicated to honoring the masculine to the decided exclusion of the feminine. It has sometimes been challenging to share openly in this environment, but gradually I have been able to step into consciously leading others to respectfully connect with and learn from nature, and honor their sacred feminine power.

Twenty-three years after starting my own journey, I can definitively state that without my reconnection to the deep, sacred Divine Feminine, I would never have been able to claim *my* full feminine power. In doing so, I've helped many people—both men and women—embrace and value the feminine truth inside and out. When a person integrates the masculine with the feminine, a wondrous healing occurs, because when these energies unite, they support powerful life creation. I love helping people find that co-creative connection between these internal forces, and apply it to their personal and professional lives.

63

I've produced products and books dedicated to helping others discover their own truth and balance, and consistently use dance as a powerful tool for reintegration, release, and activation in my online and in-person workshops. Just this year I taught a class called "Create A Financially Thriving Divine Feminine Business." It thrills me to be able to apply the elemental energies of Earth, Water, Air, Fire, and Spirit to creating and growing businesses. One of my next projects is a workshop entitled "Become a Modern Day Money Goddess: Naturally Create Your Financial Flow the Divine Feminine Way." Learning to run my finances in a uniquely feminine manner has been a huge part of my own journey.

My appreciation for the Divine Feminine in my life is tremendous, and I'm excited to say that *She* continues to be embraced by more and more people every day. Our collective experience is beginning to be more inclusive, and today there are many more books and workshops on the subject than I ever found when I started this journey.

On a recent trip to Southern California, I visited the Goddess Temple of Orange County. It is a fabulous place dedicated to honoring the Divine Feminine—a dream come true. Currently, I keep a special place in my office for images of the Divine Feminine from all over the world. I never saw images like that in my childhood, and I love surrounding myself with them now. They remind me of the special gifts and power found at the core of feminine energy.

Somewhere along my journey, someone gifted me with a very powerful CD of women's songs. I fell in love with the piece "She Speaks" by Susan Osborne. The lyrics start with *She speaks in the rushing of the river / She speaks in the crying of a child / She speaks in the glances of lovers / She speaks in the footsteps of the wild...* The underlying message of this song is that the Goddess speaks through all the precious experiences of everyday life and the wonders of natural world. I either want to dance or cry to this song every time I hear it.

I hope that you may find her—*She*—as I have, dancing in your heart, in the quiet of the morning, and in the beauty of the natural world, and embrace her. She speaks to me, and I know that if you listen, *She* will speak to you as well.

TUNE IN TO YOUR *Authentic* SELF

Where does the Divine Feminine show up in your life?

_____

_____

_____

_____

Lisa was able to reconnect with an expression of spirituality that felt more balanced to her by spending time in, and honoring the cycles of, nature. What makes you feel balanced? In what do you find aspects of both the Divine Masculine and the Divine Feminine?

_____

65

_____

_____

_____

In both ancient and modern times, dance has been used as a vehicle to honor the Goddess nature. How does dancing make you feel? How often do you allow yourself to step into the flow of free movement?

_____

_____

_____

_____

CHAPTER FOUR

AUTHENTIC
Families

Broken Up
Lisa Marie Rosati

I remember the day vividly. It was the first day of spring; the sun was shining brightly, the buds were beginning to swell on the trees, and the air smelled clean and fresh, like a new beginning. This day was also supposed to mark another new beginning in my life—and it did, but not in the way I expected.

On this pivotal day, everything I knew and depended on changed forever. It was the day I gave birth to my youngest son, Nathaniel.

I remember certain details vividly. The delivery room was decorated in various shades of blue; dark blues and light baby blues, with fake oak Formica cabinets and accents. I remember the odor of "hospital," which I loathe; it stung my nostrils. I remember the doctors and nurses popping in and out periodically to check on me, making light conversation while monitoring my contractions and pitocin drip. Finally, after twelve hours, I was ready to push. It went well: this was my third baby, so I was something of a "pushing expert." A few moments later, Nate was born.

I remember the peoples' eyes; all of them, wide open, whites huge, as they looked at one another frantically over their surgical masks. The panic was obvious.

"I'm sorry," the doctor told me. "Your son was born with a deformed right foot and leg. His right foot has three toes, and it's very small. I don't know how this happened."

69

This was so unfathomable to me that I laughed right in his face. "Ha! Stop it!" But my mom grabbed my hand, her eyes welling with tears. "Lisa, it's true," she said. I believed it then; my mother would never tell me something that wasn't true.

My next thought was, "Wait a minute. This was supposed to be a happy day!"

My legs were still up in the stirrups. I was sweaty and exhausted, but my mind wouldn't rest. I kept replaying the facts of my seemingly normal pregnancy. My son's father, and my husband at the time, was a prominent doctor in our community, so I had the best prenatal care available. Three sonograms and a late-term amnio, and every one of them was normal. How could they not have discovered this?

I wasn't the only one in shock. My husband had a breakdown right in the middle of the delivery room. He began to cry uncontrollably, hyperventilated, and almost passed out. I spent the next few days consoling *him* as I slowly went numb. The questions replayed over and over. How could this have happened? Did I do something wrong? Could the Tylenol I took at four and a half months have caused this? Why me? Why *my* child?

I never allowed myself to cry. I just sat there with a dumbfounded look on my face, trying to convince everyone else that things were "going to be just fine."

The first few months were more of the same: my husband becoming continually more detached from me and our older son, Noah, and me behaving like a Stepford Wife. Then, I moved into my "anger phase." I made statements like "Crack-addicted mothers give birth to fully formed babies all the time, and I, who did everything right, get dealt this card?" to anyone who would listen. I craved the consolation. I needed people to tell me it wasn't my fault—but the truth was that I blamed myself completely.

Even after the anger was gone, the blame continued. I had the support of my friends, my counselor, and my amazing housekeepers, but my husband continued to become more and more distant. His days at work became longer and longer, and our communication became less and less. Eventually, we ended up like two roommates—roommates who didn't even like each other.

Four short years after Nate's birth, the marriage fell to pieces. It had lasted almost ten years and produced two babies, and was the longest relationship I'd ever been able to sustain with a partner. My parents and grandparents, who had lived with me my entire life, moved out of the cottage on our property after I had an argument of epic proportions with my mom. My friends stopped coming around, because who would want to hang out with a downer like me? (Well, that, and the fact that they never knew what to say about Nate's foot.)

My Inner Critic began to pipe up, and her words stung like poison darts. "Here we go," she said. "Another failure. You couldn't make a whole baby, and now you can't even make your relationship work. You've finally become an expert at hitting the wall in your personal, professional, and love life. You're a complete loser at life! Congratulations!"

The divorce was finalized when I was thirty-nine. As far as divorces go, it went very smoothly. We hired a mediator and sat there while the last nine and three-quarter years of our lives were divided up before our eyes. During one appointment, we were both sitting there with tears streaming down our faces. "How sad," I thought to myself. "Why couldn't he have tried harder when we had the chance?"

The reality was, in my life I'd acquired several failed marriages, and now had three children to raise. I didn't know where to begin putting the pieces back together. I'd spent the last two decades as a homemaker, personal assistant, part-time interior decorator, driver, cook, laundress, and arm candy for snazzy functions. None of these roles felt fulfilling to me. I had everything that money could buy—why couldn't that be enough?

A small voice spoke to me. "Why? Because deep down inside, you know that you're destined for bigger things."

I was too fearful to step into my personal power, so I'd made it my life's work to hide behind my partner. As the voice said to me one day, while I was crying my eyes out and pleading to the heavens for answers: "You always hide behind your man."

That time, I heard the message loud and clear. It was my "Eureka" moment. I realized that part of me has always wanted to be safe from the world's judgment, from failure and criticism. The other part of me was disgusted by my cowardice. I was at odds with myself internally. When I finally connected living my truth with the thought of my happiness, it was a revelation.

72

At the same time as my marriage was ending, I took my older son Noah to Karate, and saw for the first time the weapons instructor they'd brought in to teach the class. I was instantly in love, and in lust; his shaved head, fully tattooed arms, athletic body, crisp white gi, and the quiet strength that seemed to emanate from him drew me in. I thought to myself, "Well, there's a man I'd like to get to know better!"

I did get to know him, and after a six-month courtship Mike and I were married in a small ceremony. Life was wonderful again. And out the window went my Eureka moment.

I began to fall into my old habits of neediness and clinging. I constantly needed reassurance that I was the most important thing in Mike's life. This went on for about a year—until one day, during one of our bickering matches, he turned to me and asked, "Don't you have anything you could go and do?"

It felt like he'd whacked me over the head with a sledgehammer. My ego was crushed, my self-esteem shattered. It also made the painful truth of my neediness impossible to escape. How had this happened to me… again?

I like to call this moment "The Final Insult"—the cherry on top of my dog crap sundae.

"Well, Lisa," I thought to myself. "What are you going to do now? Run away and get divorced again? Or find something productive and meaningful to do?"

I decided to find something to do. In fact, I found *lots* of things to do. I studied to become an herbalist. I got my Coaching certification, and opened my coaching practice. I completed a 200-hour Yoga teacher training. While I'd been a devotee of asana (posture) practice for fifteen years, now I began to incorporate Yogic philosophy and daily practices like meditation, Ayurveda, and breath work into my life. Tranquility enfolded me like a warm, fuzzy blanket. I discovered that the more I gave to cultivating and pursuing my own passions, the more space I created for Mike to come looking for me. It was such a refreshing change from the past scenario of me sitting in a chair, staring at him, waiting to be noticed. I'd never realized how unattractive neediness is!

73

I have finally found my life's purpose: to help others realize their truth and their power, and to discover that they are enough. By accepting myself, I have also been able to accept others. My marriage to Mike survived our trying times, and continues to get better with each passing year. My career is more rewarding and successful than I ever could have imagined. I have wonderful and close relationships with each of my three children. Nathaniel, my catalyst, is now nine, and continues to show me what courage looks like. He's already endured one leg-lengthening operation, in addition to many other less invasive surgeries. He's aware that more operations will come his way, but he takes *all* of life in stride—and if he can face life's obstacles with such courage, then I feel it's my duty as his mother to follow suit and be strong for him. Fearlessness is just one of the many lessons he's taught me.

I believe that if I put my energy into sharing what I've learned along my path, no tear I shed will have been in vain. Endless crying, feelings of despair and rejection, and utter surrender were necessary for me to understand my life lessons. Without this deep pain, I would never have faced my shortcomings and found my authentic self; instead, I would have continued on autopilot, doing the same thing over and over, sabotaging myself while each hint from the Universe got louder and louder. I have always possessed the key that could open my cage—but I had to break open and surrender to my truth in order to be free.

TUNE IN TO YOUR *Authentic* SELF

Do you find yourself repeating negative patterns in your life and relationships? Do you see these patterns as the result of others' behavior, or your own?

_____

_____

_____

_____

Lisa relied on the men she was with for validation and acknowledgment. How much of your self-worth is dependent upon the opinions and actions of others?

_____ 75

_____

_____

_____

Do you know what your life purpose is? How do you think your life and relationships will change when you find it?

_____

_____

_____

_____

Unexpected Rainbows

Nancy Fisher

*O*n a bright, sunny day in July, as I strolled with my family along the beaches of Martha's Vineyard, I felt privileged to have such a wonderful life. My incredible husband and I had enjoyed nine happy years of marriage, and he was a superb father to our three-year-old daughter, Megan. It seemed like we were living the perfect life: we both had great careers, and had just begun building the home of our dreams. Our happiness and material success was almost shameful.

Little did I know that I was heading directly into the perfect storm.

We were young enough, and naïve enough, to believe that whatever came our way wouldn't derail us, or change our destination. As baby boomers, the world was our oyster, and everything we wanted was there for the taking. We were good Christians—except that we rarely talked about balancing all the taking with giving. We believed in God, but thought we were captaining our own ship.

Fast forward two years. Our new home was nearing completion, and we continued to prosper. Then, a doctor's appointment revealed news I wasn't at all prepared for: I was pregnant! How could this have happened? I'd taken precautions! I was happy with one child. We'd planned for Megan, but I wasn't prepared for this new life. I was shocked, confused, overwhelmed, bewildered, and even a little angry.

I am the youngest of eighteen children. My mother graciously accepted fifteen unplanned pregnancies. And regardless of how she might have felt when she received the news of my coming, my mother not only accepted me but loved me as much as a mother ever could. She was my idol and my rock. The last word she ever spoke was "baby." Once I'd gotten over my initial shock, I decided I was going to follow her example. (Mom, of course, was ecstatic when I told her the news: this new grandchild would be number seventy!)

Throughout the nine months of my pregnancy, I confided to my mother all my worries and concerns. Her reply was simple, and always the same: "Trust in God, and He will provide."

I wasn't convinced.

On November 14, 1981, I gave birth to my beautiful son, Adam David. We'd moved into our new house, and I had recently quit my job due to some personal and business conflicts. I'd always been a busy career woman, but now I was a stay-at-home mom, alone in the house with two kids, sometimes for weeks at a time. It was overwhelming and lonely. Also, I felt like I was losing my business identity, and being passed over for job promotions in my absence. My career had always been an important aspect of my life, and I didn't want to see years of hard work go unrecognized because I wasn't visible.

I decided to return to the work force, but things simply weren't the same. Expectations began to take their toll. It seemed like the more I accomplished, the more the company expected from me. I felt used and under-appreciated. The contentment I thought I would regain simply wasn't showing up; in fact, I was feeling just the opposite, and the harder I worked the more disgruntled I became. The long hours and travel were negatively impacting my family. I worried that my efforts weren't making a difference in anyone's life—not even my own. After a few months of trying to find a balance, I stepped down and took a position with less responsibility.

Soon after, I noticed that Adam was not developing as quickly as Megan had. As a mother, you know when something isn't right.

Several doctors reassured me that "He is a beautiful baby, and there's nothing wrong," but I didn't believe them.

Ten months later, I finally got my answer. Adam was blind, and would likely be mentally and physically disabled.

I'd known something was wrong, but this shocked me. My pregnancy had progressed without incident. What had happened? How was I going to deal with this major roadblock to our lives? I wasn't educated in this field: how could I teach Adam the skills he would need to live if he couldn't see, walk, or talk? Suddenly, I was falling without a safety net. I'd been cheated out of a "perfect" child. I asked, over and over, "Is this how God provides?"

When I called my mother to convey the news, my heart was so heavy that I could barely speak. A devoted Catholic, my mother had always wanted one of her children to become a priest or a nun. When that didn't happen, she pinned her hopes on her grandchildren. I explained Adam's diagnosis, and when I stopped speaking she paused ever so briefly. Then, in her comforting voice, she replied, "I always asked God to send me a priest or a nun. But He went one better. He sent me an Angel."

My mother's way of embracing her authentic self was living her belief in God. She turned to her prayer book to find hope and contentment, and was my shining example of inner peace and fulfillment. "Trust in God that you have been chosen, and He will show you the way," she told me.

She was right.

I had always believed that special people are chosen to become parents of disabled children. I just never envisioned myself as being one of them. Adam wasn't a problem, and I hadn't been cheated out of anything. He was our angel. We had accepted him and loved him before we knew of his disabilities. This news hadn't changed his identity or his attitude about himself— instead, it had changed mine. I needed to shift my attitude.

Before that day, I'd been obsessed with climbing the corporate ladder in the name of the almighty dollar and recognition. The long hours, additional projects, and excessive travel were simply part of the deal. I thought my family would understand and accept the sacrifices I was making in order for us to enjoy a better lifestyle. But no amount of money or recognition was going to help my angel Adam. Only my time and devotion could do that.

I took on my new parenting role with spirit, applying all the energy I had put into my professional career. While sourcing out services for Adam, I discovered that programs for disabled children were minimal and disjointed. A lack of training, financial resources, and caregiver assistance, as well as poor educational information and social integration, meant that many disabled children were falling through the cracks.

While I could have simply sat back and complained about how the system was faulty, I decided to step in and start the process of change. I took a deep breath, and submerged myself in the process of making a difference in the lives of challenged children and their families. I explored social and education programs and services. I created parent groups and summer programs. I fundraised for camps and sports, and sourced improved occupational equipment and toys. I took on the role of an educator, and spoke to service groups, government agencies, and religious organizations. Most of all, I tried to bring families together and diminish their feelings of isolation and disempowerment.

The personal satisfaction I achieved through this work was overwhelming. For the first time, I felt I was really making a difference—not only to Adam, but to the lives of people in our community. I'd found my true calling, and my purpose. My God had given me the opportunity to utilize my talents and become a voice for those who had none.

By the time Adam was ten, he was flourishing. He'd learned how to ride a tricycle, walk with a walker, and feed himself. He was partially toilet trained, and his vocabulary had expanded to more than two hundred words. Megan adored him, and was amazing with him. Once, it had been so hard to imagine our lives with him; now, we couldn't picture life without him.

That year, I again had the feeling that something wasn't right, so we brought Adam for an MRI. We were given the worst news of our lives. Our son had a cancerous, inoperable brain tumor.

Adam had such an enormous impact on my life. Through him, I discovered my authentic self. I started out thinking that I had to teach him, but in the end, he taught me more about myself than I ever thought possible. I learned to listen, to encourage, to inspire, and to believe. I learned to love unconditionally.

Exactly two months after that MRI, God called our angel home. His mission on Earth was finished—but mine continues. By embracing my authentic self and purpose, I can inspire others to do the same. I remain constant in my faith that God will guide me to where I can make a difference in this world, and I pray that I won't miss the unexpected rainbows that come after the storms.

TUNE IN TO YOUR
Authentic SELF

Nancy discovered that her career wasn't as fulfilling as she'd originally believed. To become more authentic, she had to embrace a very different way of looking at the world and herself. Are the things into which you put your greatest energy serving your authenticity?

_____

_____

_____

_____

When Adam was first diagnosed, Nancy's initial reaction was one of shock and pain, but this belief was transformed through her faith. How can you look at your own circumstances differently? What rainbows can you discover inside the storms in your life?

_____

_____

_____

_____

Nancy writes that while she could have sat back and complained that there weren't enough resources to help her son, she decided to step in and initiate change. Where in your own life can you use your skills to create positive change for yourself and your community?

_____

_____

_____

_____

A Brave New World

Donna Cravotta

*M*y nine-year-old son Matthew is the result of a very brief relationship with a man I'll call Richard. We tried to make a go of it as a family, but we were worlds apart, and only lived together for a short time. Even living apart was extraordinarily difficult, and it was hard and frustrating and sad to watch my son carry the burden of his father's fears and irrational behavior.

Also, while Richard refused to pay child support or share any expenses, he took me to court over and over for trivial things—like preventing my son from attending birthday parties or other events on the days that were designated for his visits. I often felt that the only reason Richard wanted anything to do with Matthew at all was to have a means to get back at me.

I fastened my seat belt and prepared for another turbulent ten years. until Matthew went off to college. One of my biggest fears was that, by wishing away the craziness that Richard brought to the table, I would also end up wishing away my son's precious childhood. Whatever I tried to do to placate Richard didn't work, but I kept trying nonetheless, because I so desperately wanted a peaceful life for my son.

Last winter Richard began acting even more strangely than usual, and I became terrified for our safety. We had already been through rounds of family court, therapy, and family interventions, and I was at the end of my rope. Then came the phone call. Richard was at the emergency room, and had been diagnosed with a brain tumor.

Two days later, after surgery, it was confirmed that Richard had terminal brain cancer.

Things only became worse after that. I was not allowed to know the status of Richard's medical condition, but I did know that he was having seizures; despite this, he wanted to drive with my son and have him for overnight visits. I went to court, but the case was thrown out. I called Child Protective Services, but the social worker would not speak to Richard because he requested an attorney. I tried to speak with Richard's family, but they were no help. I was frozen with fear that Richard would harm my son, but I had no recourse. I have never felt so powerless. But it's not in my nature to give up, especially with something as important as my son's safety. I had to keep trying, even though trying was pure emotional torture.

Two weeks after the court ruled that my fears were unfounded, Matthew called me from his father's house. "Mom," he asked. "If Dad is lying on the ground, bleeding from his head, and snoring, is he still alive?" My worst fears were realized: Richard had had a seizure while alone with Matthew.

Richard came to just as I arrived at his house. I called the doctor, called his parents, and drove him to the hospital. "From now on," I said, "We go by the law of the tribal mother. If you want to see Matthew, it will be supervised. And no driving!"

Over the next several months, Richard's condition deteriorated. He spent the last four months of his life in the hospital, and eventually in hospice. I dreaded the thought of my young son watching his father die such a terrible death—but I also realized that after Richard was gone and the horror of this situation had faded, Matthew would remember my behavior. This was an important life lesson for us both, I decided. So I pulled it together, put my feelings aside, and set out to take care of a man who for nine years had worked overtime to make my life hell.

I shopped. I cooked. I took my son to visit his father almost every day. Richard's behavior was appalling. "Maybe it's due to his illness," I told myself, but I didn't really believe that. It felt as though he knew he had limited time, and had decided to condense the torture he'd had planned for us over the next decade into a few short months. I just kept smiling, and tried to get through each day. If it made my son feel good, it was worth every awful minute, and every gray hair.

Richard did not handle difficult situations well in the best of circumstances, and these were certainly *not* the best of circumstances. He was angry, afraid, distrustful of everyone around him. When we would visit, I would try to create an environment where he could have quality time with my son, but his fear was bigger than anything I could offer. My efforts often backfired, and turned into scenes from a twisted soap opera. One day, when Matthew and I visited him in the nursing facility where he'd been moved, he wanted us to take him out for a day trip. When we arrived, he was ready and waiting in his wheelchair. I found the nurse, who had all of the papers ready for me to sign. She pulled me aside and said, "I don't think this is a very good idea."

85

My instincts were in complete agreement. I suggested that instead of an outing, I could pick up lunch, and we could spend the day together here. "Maybe we can have a picnic," I suggested.

Richard was not happy. He started screaming at us, saying that we were terrible people, that he hated us, and that he was dying... On and on it went. Then, he looked right at Matthew, and said, "I never want to see you again."

The look on my son's face was raw hurt. The nurse put her arms around us and walked us out to the car. "I don't think you should come back," she said.

On the way home, Matthew told me, "I never want to talk to Dad again. He doesn't deserve for us to visit him."

It broke my heart—but we did go back after a few days, and we continued to visit Richard until his death a few months later. The funeral was terrible. We were assigned the back corner of the wake room, and we were introduced as "the mother and the son." At a time when I'd hoped we could all pull together to create a web of support for Matthew, Richard's family made it clear that they disliked me more than they loved my son.

The last blow came when I found out after the funeral that Richard had removed Matthew as a beneficiary on his life insurance policy. He'd been threatening to do this for a while, but it had been ordered by the court that he keep my son on his policy. Unfortunately, the magistrate's office dropped the ball, and never enforced the matter. I felt incredibly betrayed. It wasn't about the money. It was about the complete and utter lack of concern for Matthew's well-being that Richard displayed, right up until the last moment of his life.

I went to the cemetery, stood over Richard's grave, and told him in no uncertain terms how I felt. After holding in my feelings for so long, it was incredibly cleansing. I left many years of hurt and anger behind on that spring day, and I walked away tearful but pounds—years—lighter.

When I got home, I started a list of all the things Matthew and I were going to do, now that we no longer had to fight tooth and nail in court for the right to do them. It was kind of an "un-bucket list." As we check off items on that list, Matthew and I are beginning to undo the damage that Richard's anger brought to our lives. The fears that he instilled in my son, we are tackling one at a time: fears about heights, going on a boat, riding a roller coaster, traveling, eating new foods, sleeping over at friends' houses, and camping, to name a few.

For his part, Matthew is doing great. He's graduated from therapy, and continues to do wonderfully in school. There is a lightness to him now that was never there before. He is at peace with his dad's passing, and accepts Richard for what he was, faults and all. He's told me that he understands now why I insisted that we see his father while he was dying, even though he screamed at us and treated us badly.

I couldn't be prouder or more in awe of my extraordinary child.

For me, the months since Richard's passing have been harder. I really believed that I would feel relief when he was dead. But living with constant fear for so many years—his and my own—built up a lot of walls that I'm still dismantling. I'm letting go of the hurt little by little, so that the foundation I build for this new phase of my life will be healthy, stable, and positive. I'm trying to find compassion for Richard, who was sick with fear and anger long before he was sick with cancer. I remind myself that there is a price to pay for all things worthwhile, and that the joy of having Matthew in my life far outweighs anything that I went through with Richard.

I'm no longer the person I was ten years ago, and I'm still figuring out who I want to be in the future. Peeling away the layers of fear and anger, I'm uncovering the woman I know to be my authentic self. My story is not that of a strong woman's inspirational journey toward a fully realized goal. I am still very much a work in progress—but I am determined, tenacious, and full of hope and possibility. Each day is an adventure, and I have no doubt that I am on my way to surpassing my potential.

Stay tuned for the next chapter!

87

TUNE IN TO YOUR *Authentic* SELF

Is there a person in your life who presents you with great difficulties?

_____

_____

_____

_____

What can you learn about yourself by looking at your relationship with this person?

_____

_____

_____

_____

Often, we identify ourselves with the events or dramas of our past. How can you "peel away the layers" of your life thus far to make room for the life that's coming?

_____

_____

_____

_____

Finding Home

Rachel Larkin

*G*rowing up, I was one of those people who always had a plan. I established goals, and set out to achieve them. I was only comfortable when there was certainty in my life.

I remember my parents telling me never to marry a foreigner, as they would miss me too much if I ever left my home country of New Zealand. It was one of the few pieces of their advice I took. The irony was that, while I did marry a New Zealander, Sam was committed to living in the U.K. because of his job.

There was an ongoing discussion in our marriage about where to live. Sam loved his job, but I missed New Zealand, and at times suffered from depression. Still, we had two beautiful sons, and a lot of great times. I reminded myself that although I missed my parents and friends, my home would always be where Sam was. When our friends separated, I felt lucky that the two of us could work through anything. I couldn't even contemplate us not being together.

 89

With two young boys only seventeen months apart, our opportunities to connect as a couple became few and far between. One night, we finally managed to schedule a date, and made plans to go to the movies. For the first time in what felt like ages, it was going to be just the two of us! Holding his hand as we walked down the street, I was practically skipping, feeling like a love-struck teenager.

Sam, on the other hand, was distant and aloof. When I finally asked him what was the matter, he told me he wasn't sure he wanted to be married to me anymore, and that he thought I should return to New Zealand with the children.

I was crushed. My thoughts were a racing blur. I knew that I'd been stressed out with working and trying to run our household—who wouldn't have been?—but how had I missed this? Why hadn't I seen some clue earlier?

"Is there someone else?" I asked. "Because I don't deserve to compete with new love."

"There isn't anyone else," he assured me. "I just need some space to work things out."

I asked what I could do to help, and told him in no uncertain terms that my life was with him, and that wherever he was, I would be too. Yes, I wanted to leave the U.K., but not at the cost of my marriage.

It was all so surreal. I hadn't had a plan for this. Luckily, a friend lent me *There's a Spiritual Solution to Every Problem* by Wayne Dyer. I clung to its wisdom, and tried to focus on what I wanted. Each day, I woke up grateful to have my husband and my sons in my life.

Six weeks later, I spoke to a counselor, thinking that she might help me deal with the uncertainty. She told me that Sam's refusal to talk about the issues in our marriage was "mental torture." I didn't ring her back. Instead, I devoured more spiritual books, and started teaching myself to meditate.

Two months after that, our family went on holiday to New Zealand. I was determined to have the time of my life, despite the fact that things still weren't right with me and Sam. It was while we were away that I discovered that my husband had lied to me: he was in love with another woman.

The pain was excruciating. It ripped through me, and I collapsed in a ball of rage and disbelief. For days, I couldn't eat or sleep. Every time he left the room I was paranoid that he was calling her. It was extraordinary how powerless I felt.

But despite my overwhelming emotional response, my logical brain drove me to try to understand the situation. Sam had always jokingly called me the "research queen," and research was exactly what I did. I got four books on emotional affairs and launched my quest for answers.

The situation was incredibly tense. We agreed that Sam should return to England a month early, and that I should stay in New Zealand until our original return date. I knew he'd be running back to his new love, but I was truly committed to our marriage, and determined to find a way to salvage our relationship. In the meantime, if I could stay focused on the present moment and draw on the comfort and guidance my new spiritual teachers provided through their books, I knew I could still give my boys a wonderful Christmas.

I asked Sam not to tell me what he'd decided about our marriage until I returned to the U.K. So it wasn't until the night I flew in from New Zealand with our two exhausted children that he told me our marriage was over, and that he was leaving.

For me, part of being authentic is remaining true to your heart, regardless of what everyone else thinks. That meant that despite the fact that my husband was in love with someone else, I was going to remain committed to our marriage, because in my heart, I still felt that I was his wife.

I put myself through a marriage course, and followed the advice I was given. I learned so much during that time about my own strengths and weaknesses; it was an amazing journey of self-discovery. I felt that my efforts were going to make Sam and I stronger at the end of it all, because I was going to be a much better partner. At one point, I did ask him for a divorce—but I asked out of hurt, and realized that it wasn't a decision made from the heart.

Only after ten months of being his wife without his commitment to our marriage did I finally decide it was time to let Sam go. All the counseling and research and self-study had pulled me through, and the decision to end our marriage felt like it was finally in my hands. I arranged for us to go to dinner, and we toasted our new lives as friends.

If you really love someone, you want them to be happy with or without you. What you focus on, you draw to yourself. If you focus on love, you will receive love. I came to realize that I loved Sam as the father of our children, but no longer as my partner. It was a peaceful feeling.

The divorce went through in record time. The mediators even commented that we were a model example of separated parents. The custody arrangements were easy: we got seven days each. But I was still living in the U.K., not in New Zealand where I belonged. My life wasn't with Sam anymore, yet I was still here, and this was his place, not mine.

I told Sam that I wanted to take the boys to New Zealand for six months before our oldest started school. I also warned him that this "holiday" might become permanent, but I don't think he processed it totally, because he said, "Okay" without a single question. Maybe he just didn't believe me.

Three weeks after we arrived, the boys were having the time of their lives, and I rang Sam to say that I wouldn't be coming back to the U.K. He was shocked. He said he would come and pick the boys up; that I couldn't keep them away from him. He mentioned courts and the Hague convention. I just sent him love and meditated on a peaceful solution. In the end, he agreed that the boys could live with me, and that he would visit them over the holidays.

I realized that what I was doing was selfish. It was, in fact, the first truly selfish thing I'd ever done. But in order to be happy and live with love in my heart, I needed to be in a place that felt like home. I had to put my needs first in order to be the best and most authentic version of myself. I couldn't live someone else's dream anymore.

If it weren't for my husband leaving me, I might never have discovered my own capacity for joy in the present moment. I realize now that, while we were married, Sam loved me more than I loved myself, and that can't have been easy for him. When he couldn't do it anymore, I had to find the love within. I will always be grateful to him for the wonderful times we shared, for our children, and for the gift of uncertainty.

Today, I'm taking my life one step at a time, and trusting that it will all work out. It always does.

TUNE IN TO YOUR *Authentic* SELF

Have you ever felt that your life was being shaped or directed by someone else's actions or dreams?

_____

_____

_____

_____

Rather than let her feelings be dictated by her husband's actions, Rachel chose to stay committed to her marriage until she was ready to let it go— and discovered herself in the process. How have you responded to your own commitments when they are tested, and what have those experiences taught you about your authentic path?

_____

_____

_____

_____

Sometimes, being authentic means choosing a path that others call "selfish." In what situations do you feel it's appropriate to put your own needs first? When was the last time you did so?

_____

_____

_____

_____

CHAPTER FIVE

GROWING INTO YOUR *Authentic* SELF

Almost Forty

Kati Neal Verburg

*I*t all started with a threat.

For the nearly eighteen years that Jay and I had been married, I had been making it. I was going to dye my hair hot pink. Someday.

In our early years my taunts about the pink hair I would someday don brought about rolled eyes from Jay, as he teased me, laughing at the audacity of it all. As we aged, and our two babies turned into teens seemingly overnight, the silliness of the threat became even more obvious, and we both laughed at the idea of the middle class suburban mom with hot pink hair.

97

So, last fall when I brought up the issue as Jay and I brushed our teeth before bed, it was part and parcel that it was an immediate joke.

"You do realize that you're almost forty?" Jay teased, after my proclamation that someday I would just do it, already, and stop wasting my breath about it.

Yes, I did indeed realize I was almost forty. The age itself was not intimidating to me; I did not feel some grand sense of despair about the aging process at all. In fact, I embraced it wholeheartedly. I liked getting older. I liked *myself* getting older. Surprisingly, I was turning into a wiser person—working at *becoming* in my life, instead of being victimized by it. I was making efforts to watch my judgments of others, and of situations about which I did not know all the facts. I kept compassion in my heart, and worked to forgive both others and myself, releasing the "oldies" I had allowed to follow me around for so long. I tried to implement humility into my daily goings-on, I was recognizing that I play the biggest part in the outcome of my own life. (I'm certainly not suggesting that I always succeeded at these things—there are countless testaments to that—but I worked diligently at them, nonetheless, trying to be aware instead of habitually switching on the auto-pilot.)

In spite of all this, there was something about being over forty with hot pink hair that just did not sit right with me. And that night, with my head hung over the sink, I asked myself for the first time in the many years I'd been making the threat: "When is 'someday,' anyway?"

For years, I had convinced myself that the things I was inspired to have, do, or be, were not important enough in my now. But if they weren't important *now*, when would they become so? When would I truly embrace my Have-Do-Be?

When would I truly be *me*?

That night, I forged a deal with Jay about my hair that he would soon come to regret. For all those years, he never believed I would go through with the crazy hair color idea. But, my newfound sense of immediacy had me bargaining. The fifteen months leading up to my fortieth birthday were mine to enjoy whatever hair color I wanted. After that, I would return to the long, straight brunette style that he so loved...For *five years*. (Anyone who knows me well understands my sacrifice in that part of the bargain!) Then, we shook on it.

I didn't know it then, but this silly deal was to change me irrevocably. By stepping into my "someday," I called forth a version of myself that I had buried deep away. She emerged immediately and wholly, confident and brave. To every passer-by who gawked at my fluorescent head, I offered a wide smile, and walked away a bit taller, feeling good about embracing my uniqueness.

My hair was just the beginning. I went on a rampage of self-discovery, learning more about the woman I truly was than I ever had cared to before. For the first time, I asked questions about what I truly wanted out of life, in all areas. It wasn't long before I found myself tromping through my back story, fielding through memories in pursuit of things I had once desired, but had pushed off for another day—a day when I was thinner, or richer, or happier. Some things I recalled were nonsensical and silly. Some, I had long since lost interest in pursuing. But there were a few special someday Have-Do-Be things by which I still felt exhilarated, and I finally began accepting those exciting "wouldn't-it-be-cool-if" moments as more than empty words and pipe dreams.

I began compiling a list which I deemed my Carpe Diem Manifesto. It called me to "Seize the Day!" and embrace all of those Have-Do-Bes in order to become my most authentic version of myself. Different than a Bucket List, which focuses on things to do before one dies, my Carpe Diem Manifesto focused on things I wished to Have-Do-Be while *living*, a significant distinction.

99

I got right down to crossing things off.

Only a few weeks into my charge, I hit an inexplicable rut, inadvertently falling into the old habit of shelving my desires to connect with myself. *Without my even consciously thinking about it*, the Manifesto I had so passionately scribbled at for weeks had become another half-assed vision that I had failed to act upon. My old frenemy Complacency moved back into my life, and wrapped her stagnant security blanket around my shoulders, comforting me (and maybe even commending me) for my lack of forward motion. I was falling back into what had become real to me, and ignoring the emerging parts that spoke of a confident woman, eager and enthusiastic about continually *becoming*. Auto-pilot was winning.

My previous work to keep awareness close at hand in my life called my inaction to the surface, lighting a metaphorical fire under me, and I jumped in reaction to it. Wasn't it *me* who stamped her feet in trepidation at the long-ignored version of myself who'd lain dormant, crammed into the back of my mind, ignored and even forgotten? Wasn't it *me* who so desperately wanted to act upon my Have-Do-Bes as the most authentic version of myself? Wasn't it *me* who yelled a determined battle cry about turning my life's to-do list into my Life's To-Day list?

I could not ignore the fact that the common denominator in all of this was *me*. I realized that only *I* could take the required action to have, do, and be what I wished for in my life. I came to understand that becoming aware of this fact was merely a piece of the puzzle, and in order to create a fuller, three-dimensional picture, I'd have to make some very important choices.

Without consciously choosing, I had fallen back into my old habits of being, of feeling victimized by my auto-pilot. But control—real control of self—only comes about by making concerted choices. I needed to learn to pilot my own life, rather than handing the reins over to my subconscious. It was time for me to make conscious decisions.

First came awareness, now came choice. But was that it? Was this the magic recipe that would somehow transform me into my authentic self? I knew that it was not.

The final piece of the puzzle was *action*, and I jumped in with both feet. I shucked Complacency's heavy blanket from my shoulders and grabbed my life by the horns. I signed up for classes, delved into the development of my business, and wrote to my heart's content. I carved a path that involved both my own betterment and the betterment of those who are directly affected by my choices. I recognized and felt grateful for the love, joy, and laughter in my life.

And I am still doing all these things today—with hot pink hair.

While my hair hardly can be called the reason for my newfound sense of self-confidence and forward motion, taking that first, brave step to do something I truly wanted for myself was a catalyst which launched me toward a more secure, authentic me.

Old habits and ways of thinking knock on my consciousness from time to time, and it would be a fallacy if I said that every time they do, I make the right decision—the decision that best serves my authentic self. In these times, awareness once again comes to the rescue, thumping that metaphorical mallet up against my skull, reminding me to wake the hell up and make concerted choices. And when I listen up, and move in a direction that revives the sleepy bits of Kati...

Well, then, watch out, World, because I am *awake*.

TUNE IN TO YOUR *Authentic* SELF

What are your Have-Do-Bes?

_____

_____

_____

_____

When was the last time you allowed yourself to do something purely because you wanted to?

_____

_____

_____

_____

By taking responsibility for "piloting" her own life, Kati made a significant shift in her thinking. What are your "autopilot" habits? Do they serve who you are, and who you want to become?

_____

_____

_____

_____

Forty-Fied

Joani Plenty

"The quality of your life is the quality of your relationships."
- Anthony Robbins

*A*s my fortieth birthday approached, I decided that the Developmental Psychology Life Span Theories of Erik Erikson are not really theories at all: they're *fact*, as far as I'm concerned. It was also a fact that I was sinking quickly, in what I now believe to be the "awakening" stage.

It snuck up on me. I didn't even realize it until I was knee-deep in pre-midlife sewage! Kind of like when you grow up and have kids of your own, and one day—while standing in the kitchen with cotton in your ears and moscato in your hand, manipulating your child into behaving before you call Santa Claus, the Easter Bunny, and Cinco de Mayo—you realize that you've finally become your mother.

I joked about the subject, but only through the tears. I wrote and tried to "insert humor here," and couldn't. Like a bird singing at a funeral, it wasn't the time.

"What the hell happened?" I wondered. I was seventeen years old practically yesterday, and I'm sure that I did something literally yesterday that a seventeen-year-old would do. I could barely even spell it correctly...fourty, *forty*. I walked the same, I talked the same. I even had the same sense of humor (holding two fingers over someone's head during a picture is *still* funny). What I didn't know was if feeling mentally young was a blessing, or a curse that could possibly lead to bad choices, or a midlife crisis.

103

People turn forty every day! So why did I feel like I was the only one with the Grim Reaper on my Facebook "friends" list, just waiting to delete me? "I refuse to trade my Cocoa Puffs for Fiber One," I said to myself. "And I won't give up my sweatpants with wording across the butt for slacks or dungarees!" In fact, I've never actually owned any bold, booty-print sweatpants, but I wasn't ready to give up the option!

As you've probably guessed, forty was very scary to me. Many people fear thirty, but by the time you're thirty-one, you realize that you're actually still young, and you start looking forward to being an adult. You're old enough to demand more respect than those in their twenties, but still young enough not to be considered "old" by those same twenty-somethings. Old enough to know better, young enough to pretend that you don't.

Forty, though…Like a pimple the night before prom, it popped up overnight. And just like "Operation Blemish Annihilation" in 1989, I did everything I could think of to make it go away. I held on to my thirties like wet fingertips on a metal ice cube tray as another, slightly bigger fear reared its ugly head. I asked myself, "What am I risking by not letting go?"

As Buddha said, "You only lose what you cling to."

I was raised by my grandmother, who drove a shiny brown corvette, in a clean, wealthy, predominantly white and Jewish neighborhood. I changed friends often, as this was the nature of the childhood beast, but I had lots of friends and never felt racial limitations. I was an only child who, after making the other kids on the playground laugh with my silly antics, leaned toward the spotlight like a plant leans toward the sunny spot of a room.

I was always the one everyone called to have a good time—and for a while, that was flattering. After having my children in my early thirties I traded my heels for sneakers, glow sticks for pacifiers, and vocabulary for nonsensical words…like "nonsensical." My kids moved on to preschool and, as a stay-at-home-mom, I was at every class function; there, I met one of the other mothers, who was unhappy with her life. As time went on, we became close friends (or so I thought). She motivated me to go to the gym every day, and I lost a lot of weight. But the time spent away from my family kept increasing, bars with outdoor decks became the norm, and the "fun girl" life started to seep under the door of my home like black, poisonous gas.

My friend eventually left her husband in search of that "something" she'd missed in her twenties. Being there for her became a full-time job. But once she realized that the green grass on the single side was actually covered in poop, she returned to her marriage. The phone calls dwindled, and eventually just stopped. Saturday mornings at the soccer field with her and her husband were awkward. I could sense the tension, and realized that I'd been used as a scapegoat—as if *I'd* been the one to motivate her to leave her marriage.

105

I understood; sometimes we say or do things to smooth the bad stuff over and make our home lives as livable as possible. But her behavior pushed me toward a pivotal realization. Over the years, I'd gained and lost many friends: some to distance; some to misunderstandings; some to scheduling; and some to unexplained disappearing acts whenever I had a successful event in my life. I had what I call a "Friendship Shop." It had a revolving door, and an imaginary sign in the window that read, "No Cute Shoes, No Service." There was a firm Customer-Is-Always-Right policy which usually left me feeling like something was wrong with me and my friendship services. My "customers" would smile in my face while placing their orders, then perform acts of slander on the other side of the door. Sometimes, it got so ugly that it caused me to close up shop, and reopen elsewhere with a new circle of "customers."

Just before my thirty-ninth birthday, I sent out a mass e-mail and Facebook message regarding the big night—just as I do every year. Anyone who knows me knows that I'm not the most organized person—we right-brain thinkers usually aren't; I truly considered buying a small metal detector for the tedious daily hunt for my car keys—but I didn't want to leave the task to anyone else. This could have been because I didn't feel like I had anyone else to ask. If I didn't plan my party, who would? My childhood best friends lived miles away. Some replied to the invite with your standard Facebook "I can't wait!" but the interest level, even within myself, wasn't as high as it had been in past years. Either way, though, I was going to continue planning. My thirties were leaving me, and I was going to send them off with a bang!

I started constructing the perfect outfit in my head. The day before the big event, I primped all day. My husband Billy, after hearing of my divalicious design, said, "Why can't women just go out? Why do you always have to have a costume?"

It was going to be another eventful birthday which would leave me with swollen feet and heartburn in the works—or so I thought. The morning of my big birthday bash, nine people canceled. *Nine people*.

This was it: the moment when I began to talk to myself out loud, wondering if straightjackets came in fashionable colors. I figured no one would be more honest with me at that moment than me, so I asked the burning questions: "Is enough enough *now*, Joan? Do you see a pattern? How much time and energy are you going to put into your social life before you realize that you're taking away valuable time to pursue your goals, spend time with your family, and show your husband appreciation for his support?"

Yes. This was the "awakening stage."

I now realize that, for much of my life, I was actually drawn to the people who were the least compatible with me, whether it be for the challenge to please, to make them compatible—or worse, to sabotage myself, because it was what I was used to.

Immediately, I pulled out a piece of paper and a pen. I wrote down the names of every "customer" who had entered my Friendship Shop in the past five years in one column, their personality traits in another, and what we had in common in the last column. The similarities were astonishing. I realized that I'd spent years being bubbly and kind, confused by others' actions and the high school type cliques that kept popping up—all because I was advertising to the wrong clientele!

I celebrated my thirty-ninth birthday with just three people, and I had a blast. The next day, I sat at my computer with an overwhelming feeling of fedupness (this word needs to be added to Wikipedia pronto). "I am going to be forty soon," I told myself. "When does this end?"

That's when it dawned on me. Maybe it wasn't my thirties I was hanging on to. Maybe it was my old way of life. In that moment, I discovered the cure for Adult School-Yarditis. It's called, "I don't give a bleep." Take ten milligrams daily, and consult your physician if your heart rate increases beyond normal levels due to happiness.

Now, don't get me wrong, I take full responsibility for my part in my numerous decaying relationships. But what I've learned is that the friendships that really matter are the ones that have blossomed. I had to understand that I need a friendship niche! I can't please everyone all of the time. I need to surround myself with those who have the same interests, and who have proven that they can sustain healthy relationships, in order to keep my Friendship Shop thriving.

My pre-forty midlife crisis boiling point was suddenly reduced to a simmer.

I am in control now. I use my feelings as my guide, and no longer allow anyone to live in my head rent-free. My relationship with my husband is so beautiful, it's sparked frequent "date nights" and lots of home movie time. When I realized that the only relationships that count are the authentic ones, I found the keys to my own personal happiness.

(Turns out, they were right there in front of me, out in the open, next to my car keys.)

TUNE IN TO YOUR *Authentic* SELF

Do you dread birthdays? Do you feel that you will be required to change just because your age does?

_____

_____

_____

_____

Take a look at your "Friendship Shop." Are you happy with your customers?

_____

_____

_____

_____

What are the common traits of the people with whom you have your most fulfilling relationships? How can you use this knowledge to develop your "friendship niche?"

_____

_____

_____

_____

110

Straight from the Horse's Mouth

Kathleen E. Sims

*F*or nearly four decades, Jim and I interacted in what I call a "relationship Petri dish," learning and growing through our life experiences. I won't say we didn't push each other's buttons—there were some very challenging issues—but through it all we grew closer and closer, standing strong on the unshakable foundation of our love.

We raised two daughters, and after they were grown and gone, we enjoyed ten years free of encumbrances, and had some long-overdue fun. Then, circumstances made it necessary for us to take guardianship of our four-year-old grandson, Josh. Jim and I raised him as our own for ten years.

111

One Sunday morning, Jim stopped me in the hall, and enfolded me in a long, sweet hug. "Everyone is yearning for this kind of love and connection, Kathleen," he said to me. "And most people don't even know it exists."

Those were the last words he ever said to me. Thirty minutes later, he suffered a sudden heart attack, and was gone.

I was in shock. Being married to Jim was all I knew, all I'd ever known. I felt like I'd been given this tremendous gift, only to have it taken away.

Up to this point, my identity had been wife first, mother second, and business owner third. I felt blessed to be able to create and teach workshops on all that I'd learned about relationships and partnering during my years of evolving with Jim. It had never crossed my mind that one day I might be alone. I was fifty-seven years old, with no future financial plans and no retirement accounts. My work had only been a secondary income for our household. Childishly, innocently, I'd believed that Jim and I would live to be eighty-five together, and die on the same day; we hadn't planned for any other circumstance later in life.

My grief process seemed "doable," although I didn't cry much. I was afraid I was numb. I really missed Jim's hugs and jokes, and waited each evening for him to come through the door, but I didn't feel much pain or grief. Looking deep within, my heart was very full. I'd been so blessed to be loved by such a special man, and although he was gone, his love for me remained in my heart and soul. Nothing inside me was missing.

Harder than the grief was the identity shift I was forced to make. No longer could I be a wife first. I had never experienced completely taking care of myself—let alone taking care of children on my own. Now, I was head of household, matriarch of the entire family, and responsible for *everything*. I would have to double my income just to keep our heads above water. I was practically immobilized by the fear.

I hired a marketing coach to help me in this essential business expansion, and within a year, I met my goal. Phew! I felt taken care of—not like I had with Jim, but by Spirit.

After all that hard work, I thought I was out of the woods, and I was definitely ready to have some fun, so I bought horses. Riding in the woods and mountains with my family was incredibly therapeutic. To me, my horses represented freedom and beauty—and they didn't remind me of Jim.

A short time later, I heard about a new Equine-Assisted Growth and Learning Program, in which therapists used horses to interact with people while observing their reactions, and used those reactions as a metaphor for learning about life issues. I was fascinated, and immediately signed up for a five-day clinic. I wanted to facilitate this kind of transformational work in my own business, and this was a great way to combine my gifts of teaching and counseling with my love for horses.

At the clinic, I was asked to demonstrate one of the Growth and Learning exercises. It was simple, really: I had to try to lunge a horse. (This means standing in an arena with a horse on a rope about thirty feet long, coaxing the horse to run around you in a circle.) Owning horses as I did, I thought this would be a piece of cake.

Boy, was I wrong.

I took the rope, shortened it to about ten feet, and ran alongside the horse to get him moving at a trot. Then, I turned perpendicular to him, and started lengthening the rope so I could move back to the center of the arena. I thought he would keep moving, but every time I got about three feet further away from him, he turned to face me and stopped cold.

113

This cycle lasted a full twenty minutes—and it took place in front of about sixty people. I felt inept and embarrassed, which caused me to start laughing hysterically. I could only imagine how ridiculous I looked. I wasn't demonstrating lunging. I was demonstrating the Chinese definition of insanity: doing the same thing over and over, expecting a different result.

Finally, the counselor leading the clinic said, "Stop, Kathleen. What are you doing?"

"Trying to get this darn horse to lunge around me," I replied, humiliated.

"This horse is thirty years old, and has been lunging his whole life. Why do you suppose he won't do it for you?"

I said the first thing that popped into my head. "He likes me, and doesn't want to be too far away from me." I was shocked by my response. I felt about five years old.

"Okay. Back away from the horse, and make the rope longer."

Facing the horse (who was still standing there, staring at me), I started slowly backing up. All of a sudden, I hit what felt like a wall. I wanted to move further away, but I couldn't. I actually felt frozen in place—and burst out crying hysterically.

"What happened," the counselor asked. "Why did you stop?"

I said, "If I back up further, he will be disconnected from me, and I will die!" I knew it wasn't logical. But the feeling was intense.

The next question rocked my world. "What is this a metaphor for in your life? What are you holding on to so hard that you will die if you let go?"

The answer emerged immediately. "My husband, Jim. He died eleven months ago." The audience couldn't believe what I'd said. More, *I* couldn't believe what I'd said. I'd had no idea that I was still holding on to Jim so desperately. "If I let him go," I sobbed, "he won't know that I still love him, and he won't be able to communicate with me!"

After letting that realization soak in for a few minutes, the counselor asked me to try again. I mustered up two steps—and then hit the "wall" again.

"What is it now?" the counselor asked.

"If I move, it would be letting go of my fourteen-year-old grandson, Josh, whom I am raising. If I do that I won't be able to hear him and what he needs. He won't be able to find me!"

I was devastated to realize I was holding on so tightly to each of them. I'd really thought I was doing great in my grief process and in parenting, because I wasn't particularly sad and Josh was doing well. Now, I saw that I didn't want him to grow up too fast and leave me.

I might have hidden my true feelings from myself, but I couldn't hide them from the horse. He saw right through me, and responded in ways that mirrored my inner world. This exercise showed me the unconscious fears and beliefs that had been sabotaging my progress. The life circumstances I found myself in had created taut, invisible cords that I had attached to Josh, and to Jim in heaven. Those cords were held in place by my unconscious terror.

After that clinic, I went deep inside in prayer and contemplation. The place from which that terror originated was so deep that I could never have accessed it through a conversation—not even with a therapist. Now that I'd seen it, though, I had to unravel and heal the source of that fear, not only for me, but for Josh. And for Jim.

115

A year and a half later, having finally processed my grief and let go of my attachments, I was able to see myself in a new light. I healed my misconceptions, and finally forgave God for the loss of Jim. I realized that my authentic self isn't dependent on my life situation; instead, I see that I am an evolving Being, unfolding more of my authentic self as I grow and learn. Having shifted my identity through this transformational process, I was able to redefine my role and purpose in my relationship with my grandson. In fact, I invited all my teen grandchildren to attend one of my weekend intensives called "Live Your Vision," in which participants discover their Life Purpose and learn to live in alignment with Universal principles. After imparting this knowledge to them, I felt such freedom. They now knew how to move through the world with integrity, faith, and an open heart. My "job" is officially over: they have everything they need inside of them.

And so do I!

TUNE IN TO YOUR *Authentic* SELF

Have you ever experienced an emotional breakthrough after interaction with an animal or the natural world?

_____

_____

_____

_____

What strings have you attached to people—in the visible and invisible world—that hold you back from full self-expression?

_____

_____

_____

_____

What do you need to actively grieve in order to move forward in your life?

_____

_____

_____

_____

CHAPTER SIX

SHEDDING THE
"*Shoulds*"

Light and Dark

Kim Turcotte

I was twenty-seven when I got my first inkling of, "There's got to be something more."

It was a cold, icy February night, and my husband and I had just finished bringing in the last of the boxes from our big move. I clicked on the television while getting out the sheets, right in time to catch the tail end of a local news story. A man had just been killed in an accident on the icy roads.

When I heard that man's name, my world stood still. Could it really be that Paul, one of my best friends from high school, was gone? He'd been so vibrant, always the life of the party. I'd just seen him a few months before; we'd had a conversation about how, no matter where our lives took us, there was still some part of us that remained pals in the schoolyard.

How could someone so alive have been taken so young?

Dealing with this sudden tragedy was extremely difficult for me. But the shocking jolt of Paul's death was the Universe's nudge that cracked my life wide open, and began my journey back to myself.

Sitting at Paul's wake, all I could think was, "If I'd been the one who died, could I say I lived a happy life?" The answer was such a loud and resounding "No!" that I couldn't help but do something about it. As for what that something was…Well, in that moment, I didn't have a clue.

119

In the months that followed, I spent a lot of time thinking about Paul, and what his death meant to me. I couldn't shake the feeling that my life needed to be *more*. I started taking an inventory of my life and the choices that had created that life. What I realized was that almost every choice I'd made as an adult had been made to please someone else.

As a child, I'd been a free spirit, but free spirits weren't looked upon kindly in my house. We had structure, we had responsibility; we had models for behavior and achievement. I learned at a very young age that doing what others expect of you gets you instant approval and fewer hassles.

Even my marriage was a decision made to please others. I don't want you to think that my husband wasn't a good guy: he was a *great* guy. He just wasn't the guy for me. I knew this almost immediately after we started going out, but he'd gotten instant approval from my parents—especially from my mom, who never seemed to like anyone I dated. I couldn't understand why, if this guy was so nice and everybody loved him so much, I didn't think he was perfect for me too. I kept thinking that there must be something wrong with me.

When he proposed, I said yes, even though a little voice inside me said, "No! Don't do it!" I was trying to be the person I *should* be, something I usually measured against what my mother wanted me to be. Most things I did, I did to please her—from my choice of husband, to my job (I held the same position in the same company that she'd held at my age), to the house that my husband and I purchased from her and my dad.

From the outside looking in, I had the perfect life. But I wasn't happy, and my life wasn't perfect. I was mostly lost and lonely, and when I looked in the mirror, I felt like I didn't even know the woman staring back at me.

Paul's death, and the reflection on my life that came as a result of it, helped me take notice of how my choices had created a life I didn't really want. I spent the better part of the next year and a half in deep exploration of my Self. As a birthday gift to myself, I decided to embark on a path of change that would, eventually, let me be who I really was, rather than who others wanted me to be. It was time to shed the masks I had worn, and reveal the woman who'd been hiding behind them.

I wasn't sure how or even *if* I could change things. I just knew that in order to have even a chance for change, I had to be completely honest about exactly where I was in the moment. I bought myself two notebooks, one red and one green: the red one was for all the things I disliked about myself and my life, and the green one was for all the things I loved. As you can imagine, the red one filled up fast. I wrote pages of everything that made me feel "less than." Then, I opened the green one. It was harder to focus on what I loved about myself, but I kept at it and soon filled pages in that one as well.

121

This exercise was deeply cathartic and healing. I felt like I'd unearthed a long-lost treasure, one that had always been there but which I'd been too afraid to search for. My most amazing discovery was that the things I poured into the red book were very similar to the ones I poured into the green one. In fact, I learned that I actually loved everything about myself, even if at times I didn't like those same things! For example, I hated that I gave so much of myself away to others, leaving myself drained and resentful—but at the same time, I loved that I was generous with my time, energy, and resources.

As strange as it may sound, my experience with journaling provided my single greatest lesson in love, balance, and empowerment. I understood for the first time that everything holds light and dark; there is no good or bad, right or wrong. Everything just *is*. Knowing that, I could accept myself for everything I was—and for the first time, feel truly at peace in my world. I didn't need to change my fundamental nature; I just needed to learn to set boundaries, honor what was healthy for me, and make choices that supported who I was at my core!

When I said that my life cracked wide open, I wasn't kidding. The choices I made after discovering my true nature were all the right choices for me and my soul growth, but they weren't easy. I turned everything upside down and inside out. I left my husband of nine years, sold my house, and quit my corporate job. For a full year and a half, I enjoyed life on my terms—and finally found my bliss.

I did some waitressing and consulting work, and discovered that I didn't need a nine-to-five to feel happy or secure. Non-conventional employment allowed me to spend a lot more time outdoors, and I reconnected to my long-lost sense of spirituality. My soul was calling for some type of expression, and I became a bit of a mini-theologian. I'd been raised Catholic, but had disconnected myself from that faith in my late teens. On the one hand, God was supposed to love, accept and forgive everyone—but on the other, everything was about punishment and guilt, and women had no real place. When my research led me to Wicca and Paganism, I found the power of the Goddesses and reconnected to the rhythms of the Earth. And while I hesitate to assign myself a spiritual "label," I can say that honoring both masculine and feminine divine energy in nature, and in myself as a sacred being, is natural and empowering for me.

Of course, there was fallout from this radical departure from the safe, compliant life I had created for myself. Painful judgments came from my family and friends, and this lack of understanding led to more changes. Old friendships died away, and family members distanced themselves. But it was all okay. In fact, the space that these departures created allowed me to grow into myself. From the outside looking in, it might have seemed like my life was empty—but nothing could have been further from the truth. My life was full, and it was exhilarating.

As I stepped more fully into my life, I made new friends, healed family wounds, and met my soul mate. It's true what they say: in order to truly love another, you must love yourself first. Without the power that came from living my truth, I never would have been capable of loving another so deeply. It was from this place that I chose to marry again, this time for all the right reasons.

Married life brought with it new responsibilities, so I chose to enter back into the corporate world, promising myself that it would only be for a short while. That little voice inside me spoke up, saying, "Don't do it!"—but I let myself get caught up in the "shoulds," and ignored it.

Eight years and fifteen promotions later, I was making a six-figure salary, but I was trapped. It wasn't that I didn't like my work; I loved it, and it was easy to lose myself to the stability the job provided. But the office politics and corporate structure were feeding into my old habit of people-pleasing, so once again, on my birthday, I chose to leave my job and reclaim my life. The stability everyone else prized so highly was just an illusion if I had to sacrifice my truth to gain it.

Today, I am a successful online business strategist who helps women build their service-based businesses. I support them as they move through the process of bringing truth and purpose into their businesses. All the work I did in the corporate world fed my skill set, and I don't feel that those years were wasted—but this is the work I am meant to do, and I wake up every morning excited for the day ahead.

The lesson I've learned is that no journey is a straight line. Sometimes we move backwards, falter, get stuck, or take a detour—but in the end, as long as we remain committed to our truth, our journey will be one of peace, wonder, and love.

I still think about Paul often, especially when I'm going through a stressful situation or struggling to stay in alignment with my truth. As much as I miss him, I know that without his death I might never have had the courage to step into who I really was. I feel that our journeys are still intertwined, and that through his death, he gave me the greatest gift a friend could ever give: the help I needed to begin living.

TUNE IN TO YOUR *Authentic* SELF

Take an inventory of your major life choices. How do you feel about them?

_____

_____

_____

_____

How many of your choices were made in honor of yourself, and how many were made to please your family, friends, or partner?

_____

_____ 125

_____

_____

Kim writes that "there is no good or bad, right or wrong. Everything just *is*." What do you dislike about yourself? What do you love about yourself? How are these things related, and how can you find the balance between light and dark?

_____

_____

_____

_____

My "Cinderella" Moment

Carolyn McGee

*T*hough my father stopped drinking when I was ten, I grew up in a world where we pretended everything was always okay. We'd moved six times by then, and my father was often away, even after he became sober. My mother was overprotective, because I have a complete congenital heart block which causes my heart to work at a keep-me-alive rate of thirty to forty beats per minute. Every activity was harder for me, but I didn't want to be different, so I denied that I had any limitations. Discipline was inconsistent, and when my dad was home I tried to be the peacemaker in our house, and do everything right so I wouldn't cause problems.

127

Since I was afraid to let people know who I really was and what I thought, making girlfriends wasn't easy. I was bullied by girls who mistook my shyness for being stuck up. I needed to have a boyfriend all the time, because I couldn't stand my own company. I defined myself by whomever I was dating. I stayed in relationships that weren't healthy because I felt I had to prove that I could fix the problem. "If I only tried harder…" became my mantra.

The man I married spent our five years of dating telling me why we weren't a good fit, but my response was always to change to be what he wanted. From the outside, our marriage looked pretty and happy. We both had good jobs, we owned a nice house, and had two healthy children. But from the beginning I'd given away my inner power to him—so much so that there was really only one person in the relationship: him. I wanted to be loved so desperately that I became whomever and whatever he wanted me to be.

But the person I was didn't match the person he wanted. I am very social, and love entertaining and going out with friends. He wanted me all to himself. "If you loved me," he'd say, "you wouldn't want to go out with people from work. You'd want to come home to me." He was often up well before 6:00 a.m., but couldn't stand to be alone, so he'd badger me until I got up, too.

Before we got married, he told me that if I ever weighed more than he did he could divorce me. When we went to the gym, he would walk by the Stairmaster to see if I was working at a high enough level for him. If he didn't like my speed, he'd change it, despite my struggling heart. Instead of standing up for myself, I would just lower the speed when he walked away. When I was pregnant with our second child, we had family in town, and I brought home ingredients for ice cream sundaes. The day before our family left, he threw out all the leftovers, so I couldn't eat them and get fat.

Everything was under scrutiny: my weight, my looks, even the clothes I wore. Every day, I endured his sarcastic comments. My way of dealing with this was to keep changing whatever was wrong until there were no more comments. But he was never happy, and neither was I. When he withdrew and gave me the silent treatment, I relived my childhood abandonment. When we disagreed, there was no compromise.

Eventually, I stopped trying. Instead of putting my energy into one-sided discussions, I gave in, and gave up my soul.

I lived in a gray world of others' expectations, forgetting that I had any myself. My work was demanding, and I thrived there, because I felt respected and accomplished. But the better I did there, the worse things got at home. My husband resented the extra time and energy I was putting into my career, and pressured me to spend more time at home. Eventually, I became physically ill from the stress. I went through a period of complete emotional shutdown. I was lost.

I saw the first glimmer of my internal light when my son was six months old. I had just been promoted, and was under a lot of stress at work. To top it off, I thought I might be pregnant again.

When I told my husband, his response was, "I can't have another child. You'll have to get rid of it."

Something inside of me flickered into life. "Maybe you can't," I told him. "But I might."

As it turned out, I wasn't pregnant, but standing up for that life—a life I hadn't even been sure existed—gave me new energy.

A few months later, I had my epiphany.

One Sunday morning, I awoke to the news that Princess Diana had died. Even though I didn't really understand how lost I was, I related to her struggle to be herself and find personal happiness, and realized that she had only begun to step into her power and live her life when she died. By living someone else's version of my life, I was showing my daughter that it was acceptable to make someone else happy at her own expense. I had to break the cycle.

As I cried for Princess Diana, I wept for myself. I felt the small flame that had ignited months before catch fire. I was determined to regain my life and live as God intended me to, whether or not my husband liked it.

I started talking to people about the reality of my life, instead of giving them the pretty version of things. I called my parents and asked them to stay with me for support. I asked my husband to change marriage counselors when I wasn't comfortable with his choice. I started wearing clothes that I liked, and eating what I felt like eating. Although it made some people unhappy, and I lost some friends along the way, I began to make choices based on what was best for me. I realized that I am not answerable for the way anyone else feels—not even the man I married.

My marriage couldn't survive without my playing a passive role. It tore me apart to end the illusion, but I had decided to be me, and there was no going back. I filled the void inside me by voraciously reading books by Abraham-Hicks, Suzanne Somers, Doreen Virtue, Louise Hay, and Dharma Khalsa. To better understand my background, I re-read books about growing up in an alcoholic home. I found a wonderful therapist and went back to church. I read about life beyond death.

While I was still trying to patch things up with my husband, my deceased grandmother was with me strongly. She had been an avid gardener, and when I was sad I would smell sweet flowers and feel her hug me just as she had when I was a child. Her pure love enveloped me. My husband told me I was crazy—until the night he smelled the flowers, too. He got up and ran around the house checking all the windows and peering into every corner. I laughed: it was just my grandmother, protecting and encouraging me.

After my divorce, I met a psychic who helped me start my voyage toward my spirituality. By learning to meditate, I reconnected to my long-suppressed intuition and began following the guidance I received. In the past, I'd been a perfectionist, and would get frustrated when I was not successful at everything I tried. Now, my perspective had changed, and I experimented with many different things. I read Tarot cards and Runes. I learned how to use crystals to clear the energy of a room, and used Feng Shui to decorate my home. I became a Reiki Master.

Every book I read and class I took brought me closer to the understanding that I am a strong, intuitive woman, and have always had an incredible connection to the Divine. My life's purpose wasn't to serve others at my own expense, but to use my gifts to help others while standing strong in my own power. I went from fearing life to accepting that life is good—and, more importantly, so am I!

When my high-tech job was downsized, I took the opportunity to start a pet care business. My intuitive connection gave me an advantage with the animals. I knew this wasn't my true path, but I loved the flexibility of being more available for my children, and I used the space to learn and grow.

It was the classes through AngelsTeach that truly brought me back to myself. I learned to acknowledge that my inner voice is my connection to my source and my angels. Communicating with my angels and discovering a wonderful community of light workers showed me where I belong. Today, as a spiritual teacher and Angelic Life Coach, I guide others to embrace their inner power and rediscover the path they may have wandered from.

During a meditation, I experienced my "Cinderella" moment. Archangel Michael escorted me into a coach made from a pumpkin, and I knew I had transformed my energy and was ready to step into my power. I wasn't downtrodden and hiding in a corner anymore: I was on my way to my own personal ball to have the time of my life!

My life has been an amazing journey, and every relationship I've had has been a gift. If I hadn't lost myself in unhealthy relationships, if I hadn't had my ego stripped away, I would never have reclaimed my child-like innocence and connection to Spirit. Now, I stand in my own power and live my life authentically. Through my experiences, self reflection, and connection with the Divine, I can now be of service to others without sacrificing who I am.

TUNE IN TO YOUR
Authentic SELF

Carolyn writes, "I defined myself by whomever I was dating." Have you ever stepped out of your authenticity in order to please your partner or spouse? Why did you feel this was necessary?

_____

_____

_____

_____

Do you often find yourself painting a picture of your life that glosses over the reality? What do you feel would happen if you told the unvarnished truth?

_____

_____

_____

_____

Have you experienced a "Cinderella" moment? What did your transformation look like?

_____

_____

_____

_____

Surrendering the Veil

Cathleen O'Connor

"Hard times arouse an instinctive desire for authenticity."
- Coco Chanel

I remember clearly the day of my First Communion. My mother, distracted by an argument with my father, forgot to bring my communion veil with us to the church. Neither she nor the two kind nuns could console me. I cried my way up the aisle wearing a black mantilla one of the nuns lent me, feeling deep embarrassment and shame.

To understand that little girl in that moment you have to understand the emotional chaos that surrounds an alcoholic family. By the age of seven, I had already abandoned myself to focus on the emotional caretaking of my parents—especially my father, because his was the addiction. My father wasn't there that day to see my communion, and his absence somehow got all tied up with the missing veil. I was crying not just for the loss of a piece of clothing but for the greater loss of a family that would never be what I needed.

By age ten, I had gotten my approach to life down. If I could just meet others' expectations for who I *should* be, I would be accepted and loved. So I put all my energy into outward achievement, the one area that seemed to bring the positive attention I found nowhere else. I was a great student, with the ability to effortlessly learn, and I used that skill to excel in high school, college, and my first "real" job as a computer programmer.

My skills eventually took me all the way to a position as Vice President of Technology for a global pharmaceutical company. By then I was an expert at figuring out what others expected, and that ability served me well in my corporate career.

From the outside looking in, I was a complete success. I had a wonderful career, a fabulous Manhattan apartment, and the financial resources to live a life of carefree independence. From the inside looking out, I felt empty, and filled that emptiness with a jam-packed schedule, shopping, and emotional eating.

As I approached my late thirties, the inner pain of my life pushed me into working with a therapist who helped me understand the roots of my depression and lost sense of self. At the same time I began a study of spirituality in earnest. I wasn't drawn to organized religion, but had always been interested in the spiritual path. Throughout my forties, I met monthly with a group of fellow spiritual seekers and began to develop a new view of my life and myself. These two tracks of self-healing—conventional therapy and spiritual development—gave me the courage at age fifty to leave my corporate job so I could focus on creating a career more in alignment with the new beliefs and self-realizations I was experiencing. What I most loved in my career was mentoring others, and I wanted somehow to incorporate my natural skills as a counselor and mentor into my next venture.

I made a lot of changes that year. I moved from the city to a suburb. I attended art classes, singing lessons, and writing seminars. I obtained a PhD in Metaphysical Counseling. Through this process of change, I began to get back in touch with my essence as a co-creative force in my own life.

Yet, the inner emptiness still haunted me. As I made this important life transition, I again began struggling with my old nemesis: depression. My sense of personal identity was very tied up with my corporate position and all the trappings of success that came with it. Without my title and career to define me, I wasn't sure who I was. In order to calm my anxiety, I rushed into opening my holistic wellness center, hiring staff and draining my financial reserves.

While I loved my counseling and teaching work, the larger business structure of a healing center and gift shop was not financially viable. Two years in, I knew the business was in trouble—and yet, I couldn't seem to take the steps to admit it wasn't working. My life-long pattern of focusing on the expectations of others over the reality of my own needs kept me heading down a road that continued to drain me financially and emotionally. I juggled madly to keep the business afloat while managing a gnawing anxiety that what I was propping up was going to collapse at any moment. I hardly slept, and completely lost touch with my own intuitive voice.

Finally, I secured a buyer for the business. It seemed as if I was going to make it through my crisis after all. And then, two events occurred. First, the landlord of the commercial building that housed my center sold the space out from under me, causing my buyer to withdraw. Second, payments from an ill-advised business loan I had made stopped coming, and the loan went into default.

And that is how I found myself sitting in the offices of a bankruptcy attorney on one sunny October day with a box of tissues by my side, wondering how on Earth I had gotten to this place.

What I didn't know as I sat with the bankruptcy attorney was that this was exactly the opportunity I needed to get real about my life and myself. A bankruptcy is actually a rebirth: the debts of the past are cleared away, and everything starts over. As I realized that my situation was a metaphor for rebirth on a much grander scale, I remembered the Phoenix which rises from its own ashes, more beautiful than before, and empowered with the knowledge that anything is possible.

What I felt sitting in that office was shame and embarrassment. Once again, I was that little girl in church, wearing the nun's black mantilla. I'd come full circle: I couldn't escape that part of myself any longer.

The bankruptcy was a humbling experience, but it also flowed directly out of patterns from my past that had finally caught up with me; the culmination of a pattern of self-neglect that was rooted in my alcoholic family. All the achievements of my professional career couldn't compensate for a lack of self-value so great that I literally gave my *self*—and my resources—away. Now, the opportunity was before me to strip away the veil of success and achievement and delve into the deep healing work needed to reclaim my authentic self, flaws and all.

As I worked on myself, I had to learn how to establish healthy emotional boundaries, and let go of my tendency to emotionally and financially "rescue" others. After a lifetime of over-giving through lavish gifts, loans, time, and resources, I was finally learning how to receive. I learned the power of saying "No" when faced with demands that aren't consistent with my own needs, and the importance of saying "Yes" to myself and my dreams.

My authentic self is a woman who can look at her flaws without flinching, celebrate her courage, and do the difficult work to reclaim all that she is. My bankruptcy forced me to walk the talk I had long espoused: that my life is, first and foremost, a journey of spiritual discovery. As I healed, I moved through deep grief, anger, pain, and hurt, and found my way at last to an acceptance of all that I am.

I continue to redefine success for myself on a daily basis with meditation and a creative writing practice which led me to a publishing contract for my first book. Over the last few years, as the economy has struggled, I've found myself counseling others through the bankruptcy process. Ah, the Divine Hand at work. There are no mistakes: I was given exactly the experiences I needed to be able to offer support, guidance, and compassion years later to those who need it. I've been able to say to them with certainty that this event, however difficult, is the right choice; that they will get through it, and emerge on the other side to find new meaning in life.

Today my life brings me gifts of peace, calm, and joy. Through my healing process, I learned that I actually have very little attachment to material things—that I can be happy with just the basic necessities. My gratitude for the beauty of my life and my creativity is a greater and more constant source of joy. I now mentor other women entrepreneurs, write articles and books, and speak and teach on the alchemy of transformation and awakening to the authentic self. I know my life is on exactly the right path, whether or not I can see where that path leads. Now, my outer success is a perfect complement to my inner success: a picture of a life of purpose, passion, and joy.

TUNE IN TO YOUR
Authentic SELF

Often, our adult lives are reflections of the emotional lessons we learned in childhood. Cathleen continued her pattern of caretaking at her own expense long after she'd left her parents' home. What residual patterns do you see in your present situation? Are they authentic to the person you are today—and if not, what steps can you take to change them?

_____

_____

_____

138 The life challenges that shake you to your core are also the challenges which present the best opportunities for growth. When was the last time such a challenge showed up for you? What did you learn from it then? What can you learn from it now?

_____

_____

_____

Cathleen discovered after her bankruptcy that she hadn't been "walking her talk," living the life of spiritual purpose she'd been seeking to guide others toward. Do you practice what you teach?

CHAPTER SEVEN

_____

_____

_____

BACK TO BUSINESS:
Authenticity
IN ACTION

The Open Window

Gayle Joplin Hall, PhD

*I*n 2005, I was a divorced mother living in a relatively small town in Texas, and had been raising my son Taylor alone for the past eight years. In our community, good jobs were scarce, and I felt fortunate to have a better-than-average income.

One of the requirements for my corporate job was frequent travel. Being an excellent mother and making a respectable life for my son were my top priorities, but during 2005, I was away from home one hundred and twelve days. Taylor, who was fourteen at the time, wanted to stay alone; however, there was no way that was that going to happen in my strict Christian home, so I hired a nanny from our church to stay with him during my absences.

I enjoyed the national accounts I called on. Nevertheless, my heart ached every single time I left town. Taylor never liked it when I was gone. If you asked him, he would declare that I was gone "all the time," instead of less than one-third of that year. I truly never realized his pain, but I undoubtedly felt mine. I was only cheerful on Sundays when, after Taylor and I went to church, I could perform my volunteer work, tend to my flowers in the backyard, swing on my porch with Taylor while watching the dazzling sunset, or jump on my Harley for a nippy evening ride.

On Friday, December 16, 2005, at 7:45 a.m., the company President came into my office, and asked me if I could stay a little late after work. As he exited, I guzzled the remainder of my coffee, and felt a pit open up in my stomach. I was going to be fired at the end of the day. I just knew it.

141

I immediately called my father and told him my gut fear.

"Sis," he said. (He always calls me "Sis" when he's serious.) "The writing is on the wall. You're the top one in sales, and the company has new owners again. It's easy for them to get rid of you. Brace yourself. You're a Hall. You'll be fine."

He didn't console me, or tell me what I wanted to hear. He simply confirmed what I already knew.

At 5:00 p.m., I walked into the President's office. He would not look at me. Here sat the man with whom I had laughed so many times, the man who had applauded me for my big sales, and he could not look me in the eyes.

With his bald head dripping with sweat, he said, "Gayle, I don't know how to say this, but I have to let you go. We pay you a lot of money. We are going to be making many changes, and those changes are starting with you."

"What did I do wrong?" I asked.

"Absolutely nothing."

"Then how can you fire me? How can you do this to me a week before Christmas? I'm a single mother!" He had to know the burden this would put on me and my son.

His eyes welled up. "I know you're frightened, Gayle," he said, "But I have a feeling you're going to come out on top of the world."

When I got in my car, the first thing I did was scream. Then, I cursed. I almost wrecked the car twice on the way home, because I was fuming. I called my parents, crying hysterically. What was I going to do for money? How was I going to make my mortgage payments?

When I pulled up to my house, I was still sobbing so hard that I could barely tell Taylor the news. I did not want for him to be afraid, but I was terrified beyond belief. He relied on me for everything. I called a neighbor and asked if Taylor could spend the night at her house. I didn't want him to see what I was going through.

Ten minutes later, Taylor was gone, and I was alone. I dragged myself into the sunroom, where my beautiful canvases of angels were hanging, and got down on my knees. I prayed to my God, but no answers came. I meditated, and listened to my fountain of running water. I read poetry. I pored through my art books, although I didn't know what I was searching for. I closed my eyes and begged God to speak with me. I asked Him why a good person like me would get fired.

Still, no answers came. I had been in my sunroom for four hours.

Then, I had an inspiration. A hot bath. Yes, that would help. A hot bubble bath filled with the scents of roses and vanilla sugar. Those luscious aromas might help me feel better.

I undressed, lit my seven candles, and climbed into my brimming tub. As I slid down into the water, I watched the flickering flame of one candle start to dance. None of the other candles' flames were dancing like this one.

I quickly realized this was the prelude to God's message to me. This was going to be my moment of learning from God! The feelings of nervousness, anger, and fear disappeared from my soul, as though they'd become transparent. I had not been in the bathtub for even five minutes.

The message from God was crystal clear and flawless. God explained to me that I had been unhappy ever since I had begun traveling for a living. The images were distinct: I could actually see myself dragging my suitcase in and out of rental cars, checking into hotels late at night, calling Taylor from the road. I was so tired of it all. Most of all, I was tired of not being able to spend my time doing what I loved to do: helping other people.

I never heard God's voice speaking to me out loud. It was more like the angels from my beautiful paintings in the sunroom were flying around, soulfully singing to me with His spirit and His words. God expressed His desire for me to spend more time doing the things I love—like sharing time with Taylor, volunteering, and helping other people. He explained to me that although I had been making a living, I had not been living my life in the way I needed to in order to be satisfied. I was not using all of the talents with which God had blessed me. I had been phony, just to pay my bills. As a result, I felt empty most of the time, searching for more, wanting more.

God stated that I should be speaking, writing, teaching on many levels, and assisting others, instead of working in a corporate sales job. Yes, I was earning a living, but I was not contributing to society or helping anyone.

The next thing I knew, I was soaring out of the bathtub. I ran with wet feet into my bedroom, opened the nightstand drawer, grabbed my tablet and pen, and started writing. I could barely scribble the words down quickly enough. You see, when an "ah-ha" moment of insight learning hits you, it is like the lights have been turned on after you've been in the dark for years.

My note pad was full before midnight, and by the time my head hit the pillow, I knew exactly what I was going to do, and the steps necessary to make it all happen.

They say that when God closes a door, He opens a window. My being fired was a window of opportunity opening—God's way of telling me that it was time to move away from this small town to a bigger city. My dream was to teach at the college level, and there were no university positions in Psychology available in our little town. In the city, I could earn my PhD, get a professorship, and follow the authentic life path God had shown me.

In order to accomplish this without my old source of income, I calculated that I would have to downsize by at least seventy percent. The next day, I put my home on the market. I organized an estate sale, where I made $11,000 in pre-sales and over $4,000 from my sunroom sale. After my home was sold, I was left with $93,000 in cash.

Yes, God is good. You just have to be willing to accept His changes when they come. I lost a lot of my material goods, but I gained the freedom to follow my calling.

Taylor and I lived in a little rented house for six weeks so he could finish out the school year, and then I found a home in Dallas. I chose this magnificent city in part because my very good friend, who was diagnosed with breast cancer shortly before I lost my job, lived there, and I wanted to be nearby to provide comfort and support. After I'd settled in, I found a way to take full-time credits and earn my doctorate in Psychology while teaching college courses at the same time. My dissertation was about domestic violence and therapists, which is my area of expertise.

This year, I have taken a sabbatical from teaching to start my new Happiness Life Coaching business, write a book, present as a keynote speaker, and guide people toward finding the kind of fulfillment and happiness that God has made possible for me in my own life. My old boss was right: I have come out on top of the world.

You see, I know that God has big plans for me to help people. And as long as I remain on my authentic path, there will always be an open window.

TUNE IN TO YOUR *Authentic* SELF

Have you ever heard the voice of your higher power? What did it tell you?

_____

_____

_____

_____

Only when Gayle's mind was calm was she able to hear the voice of her God. If you have trouble hearing your inner wisdom speak, how can you create a quieter space in your mind?

146

_____

_____

_____

_____

Big changes—like selling off seventy percent of your material goods—can be difficult, and we often resist such changes when they come. Have you ever been asked to give up material things to which you were attached? Were you able to do it?

_____

_____

_____

_____

Back to the Middle

Catrice M. Jackson

*E*ager to make my dream to transform the lives of women around the globe a reality, I chose to try a different path—only to find myself feeling awkwardly disconnected in the midst of brilliance.

In retrospect, I should have stayed in my own lane, but after watching so many other business owners excel overnight, I decided that I too wanted a piece of that success. So I decided to hop over to the fast lane and give it a try. Before I knew it, I was cruising recklessly down Illusion Highway, headed out into the middle of nowhere.

And then, a wake-up call. I collided with another racing businesswoman who told me in a very nice way, "You're not ready for the big lanes. You need to drive *big*, or get off the track."

147

Shocked and slightly offended, I pulled up short. I was at a loss for words—which is rare for someone who loves to talk as much as I do. As I hung up the phone on our mastermind group call, I wondered, "How the heck did I get here?"

Just months before this spiritual collision, I'd been excited to join our mastermind group, which included some amazing women whom I respect and adore. Our juices were flowing, and we were eager to begin blending our brilliance into a masterpiece of success. I just knew I was going to receive what I'd been searching for personally and professionally: fabulous female connections with women who were serious about taking their businesses to the next level. Our monthly sessions started out with a bang, and soon we were strategizing and sharing ideas for rapid, resounding success.

Early on, my intuition started whispering, "Are you sure this is where you need to be?" My ego responded. "Yes, absolutely! These women are hungry for success, and so am I!"

Have you ever wanted something so badly that all you could see was the glitter and shine? Have you ever thought, "This is the one thing that will take me where I want to go right now," and hopped right on the bandwagon? Have you ever been so hungry for something that you gobbled up just about anything that so much as smelled like what you were craving? My answer to all three of these questions was *yes*! I had been working in my business for about three years, with bouts of success and failure. Everywhere I turned, there was some guru touting the magic formula for success. My entrepreneurial journey began to feel more like a day in a theme park. I longed for the ease and grace of the merry-go-round, but I was blinded by the pretty lights and the roaring speed of the roller coaster.

My ego wasn't helping things any. It justified its desires to me with wooing statements like, "You've worked so hard. You deserve this. You're ready to play big now, and it's time to get paid. You deserve all the bright and shiny things you want." These thoughts were like drops of nectar on my tongue. My ego was right: it *was* my time. I deserved what these other women were finding. I'd certainly worked hard enough to earn it.

Some people will tell you that great minds think alike. I'd more confidently say that *like* minds think alike. Everyone has greatness within them, but someone else's greatness might not be a good match for yours. The power of masterminding lies in a circle of like minds, and it's a powerful place to be and grow personally and professionally— when it's in alignment with who you are and what you believe in.

What I craved was soul-satisfying work. What I was getting was a marketing pitch. Our success sessions seemed to be deeply anchored in making money fast, securing high-paying VIP clients, list-building, and selling. While it all sounded egotistically yummy, it felt spiritually sour. I'd worked all my life as a counselor and advocate. Yes, I wanted to make a good living for my family, and fuel my personal and professional dream of traveling the world as a sought-after speaker and best-selling author. But I had never seen myself as someone who chased the Almighty Dollar.

Shortly before my spiritual collision, I was encouraged to set up a sales page using a template created by a well-known, highly paid speaker and coach. The other ladies in the mastermind group were sharing how well this strategy had worked for them, and how it would work for me. But this strategy just wasn't resonating with my spirit. In fact, I felt dis-ease in my soul just thinking about implementing it. Waves of defensiveness rose up in my body. I started to debate with the rest of the group. That was when one of the other "drivers" told me I was playing small.

My ego, wounded, prompted me to set up the template, despite the feeling of deceit I was carrying. I published and promoted it, with little success. I wasn't really surprised. The next time we met as a mastermind group, the driver with whom I'd collided suggested that we discontinue the group. I immediately agreed. After we wrapped up the session, I sat back and sighed, feeling like a ton of bricks had been lifted from my spirit. I had lost my focus, my voice, and my soul purpose in the pursuit of bright and shiny things. Now, it was time to get back to the middle—to my place of peace, harmony, truth, and authenticity.

Over the next couple of months, I learned that I'd been placing too much value on whether I had the "right" clients or speaking gigs. I'd been letting these results determine my value, wealth, and worth. Now, I stopped following those amusement park gurus. I listened to my inner voice instead, and decided to trust God, my Source, to provide the resources and financial opportunities I needed to create success.

This journey wasn't chronologically long, but spiritually it seemed to take forever. I felt alone and confused, unsure of what my next steps should be. I spent many moments in prayer as I sought answers, direction, and guidance about how to live and work more consciously and authentically. While in that valley, I faced many of my fears about both failure and success, and slowly, I reconnected with my soul's purpose: to inspire other women to live bravely and authentically. I'd been censoring my message, trying to follow the pack. When I recommitted to this calling, I felt liberated. I remembered that my business wasn't just about me, and what I could get from it; rather, was about the women whose lives I could transform by following my path. I was able to redefine success on my own terms, and connect with other women in business who shared my vision. I will never again lose myself in the process of chasing dollar signs—because by doing so, I took my eyes off the Source of my true prosperity.

I wanted to live my dream bigger than I could imagine, and in doing so, allowed my ego to reign. Now, I've revived my "SHero," the wise, intuitive source within, and I've given her full permission to teach me how to say no, and when to say yes. She whispers two very powerful words to me—"So What"—and encourages me to use them often. *So what* if my message is different? *So what* if I'd rather blaze a hot new trail than follow the beaten path? *So what* if I express my sassy, feisty personality, and *so what* if some people don't like it?

Never again will I lose sight of my God-given luminosity, or allow another to define my shine. The more I show up authentically, the more I am affirmed by my friends, family, fans, and followers. I'm enjoying the ride of my life—not on the roller coaster, but on the merry-go-round. Sure, there are ups and downs, but I flow with them, and allow the ease and grace of my middle ground to keep me humble, mindful, and authentically *me*.

TUNE IN TO YOUR *Authentic* SELF

Have you ever felt pushed, in life or business, to follow a road that feels unnatural or inauthentic to you?

_____

_____

_____

_____

When you've stepped off your path to pursue the "bright and shiny," what were the results?

_____

151

_____

_____

_____

The two words given to Catrice by her SHero, "So What," have been incredibly powerful in her life. Where in your own life can you say, "So What?" How would it feel?

_____

_____

_____

_____

152

Life on My Terms
Shann Vander Leek

"It's never too soon, nor too late, to follow your passion."
- Shann Vander Leek

I woke up in a dreadful fury. The red light on the alarm clock glared at me: 5:30 a.m. A few more minutes of sleep was all I wanted—anything to put off going back to the office.

Does this sound like your average day? It used to be mine.

For many years, I had enjoyed my job, but now it felt more like a prison sentence, and I knew I had to find a way to escape. Somewhere along the way, the corporate culture I was immersed in had changed to a game of ego-driven micro-management, and I began to experience a slow and certain suffocation. It was time to get real, face my fears, develop a critical path to transition, and become the mistress of my own destiny. But how?

153

I was already getting several strong signals that it was time to make a change, but I guess it's hard to recognize when you're just "bumping around" while you're still bumping around. I remember feeling confused, fearful, angry and scattered. The pain of an uninspired work life lent itself to a reactionary autopilot protection program that only made things worse. I was just going through the motions, no longer feeling challenged by, or even interested in, the duties I once loved. Many days began with the dreaded alarm clock and a state of anxious dread. I was unnerved by the decisions my corporation was making, and felt like a fish out of water in what used to be a very comfortable environment. A recent regime change had taken me from a state of near autonomy to one of micro-scrutiny. In other words, I went from being the golden girl to a cover girl with a giant pimple.

There was no way I was going to jump through flaming circus hoops just to get a paycheck. The job was killing my soul, and I needed to find a way out.

I went through many phases of self-examination, doubt, fear, and suffering before I finally realized it was time for a significant change, but my epiphany came during an uncomfortable board meeting with our newly appointed, ego-driven, general manager. Just two years prior, I'd been rewarded with a trip to Scotland for my leadership efforts and double-digit revenue growth. But then, the economy tanked, and someone had to pay. That someone, apparently, was me. The game of the day was, "Break the sales manager, then build her up again." Angry and out-of-control, I let him have it. It was not a pretty sight. And, I did it in front of several witnesses, all of whom were men.

Ugh. It was a disaster... But I digress; on to the epiphany.

While all of this madness was in progress, I happened to look out the window. All day, it had been dark and stormy—a perfect match for the climate in our boardroom—but now, one of the most marvelous rainbows I've ever seen was shimmering across the sky. I knew I was the only person in the room who could see it. It was as if it had appeared just for my eyes.

At that moment, I knew I was going to move on, and that I was going to be okay.

Today, I understand that without the extreme discomfort my former work environment caused, I might have never allowed myself to embrace my true passion and follow my dreams—but at the time, it was, to put it simply, hell. The first phase of any significant transition is very uncomfortable, and mine was no exception. An enormous shift was coming, and I could feel it. I could taste it. But even after I saw the rainbow, I couldn't quite wrap my head around it. All I knew was that the more I tried to fight it, or think about things "logically," the more I felt trapped in that place of discomfort.

A large percentage of the eight-to-five workforce seem to have accustomed themselves to a certain amount of suffering. It's as if people are trying to buy security with the currency of their own pain. But we can't live for the promise of a day in the future. When I discovered that security was an illusion—that all my hard work and sacrifice hadn't even bought me a place in the new corporate regime, let alone a ride to retirement—happiness became all that mattered. Did I want to spend my life making a life, I asked myself, or dancing in a cage for a paycheck? The answer that came to me was this: I was no longer willing to put my life on hold for the sake of a company I didn't believe in.

Another sure sign of my need to transition was the feeling that I simply must *make* a difference in the world. The fat paychecks and benefits were no longer enough. A major turning point for me was my realization that selling television commercials does absolutely nothing meaningful for the world. Advertisers spend gobs of money to promote products like Viagra and Lipitor, so that the general public can keep an erection and eat cheeseburgers. Wow! When I stepped back to think about what my job really entailed, I discovered that I was no longer willing to be part of an organization which had no interest in a healthy corporate culture, which was teeming with politics, and which had no interest in human kindness.

This wasn't an easy truth to swallow: I had invested much of my life in the television advertising business, and I loved the game—until I didn't anymore. Hey, people change.

To make my great escape, I had to focus on what I needed to get from Point A to Point B. I knew that I wanted to earn my professional coaching certification, and that I needed to get clear about my finances and save some money to cover household expenses before taking the leap. And that was pretty much it. I didn't have a niche market. I didn't have clients. I only had the knowledge that what I was doing wasn't authentic to me anymore.

I decided to take my time, so I could really wrap my head around the idea of leaving the only career I'd ever known. It was both amusing and disheartening to realize that all my dedication, smart work, and energy—all the things I put into my career every day—were given only for the sake of receiving a paycheck, but this awareness helped cement my corporate world exit strategy. I had to let go of the illusion of control my leadership position and fat salary created.

And so, after fourteen years with the same organization, and eighteen years in the television advertising industry, I found the courage to let go on my terms. I packed my box, said "so long" to the big bucks and my cushy expense account, turned in my pimped-out company SUV, and walked away from a career that no longer suited me.

Today, I'm grateful beyond measure that I had the courage to follow my conviction. Letting go of my ties to the corporate world allowed me to create an international coaching business dedicated to supporting powerful women in transition who wish to accelerate life on their terms, and create more balance in their lives. All of the characteristics that made me a success in the advertising arena benefit me now as an entrepreneur. I have a healthy family life. I've traveled to many delightful places. I live in the home of my dreams. I've become a successful entrepreneur, yogini, and published author. And I am eternally blessed to have the opportunity to be true to myself, follow my dreams where they lead me, and support others as they do the same.

Because it's never too soon, or too late, to follow your passion.

TUNE IN TO YOUR *Authentic* SELF

Is your current career serving your purpose and passion?

_____

_____

_____

_____

Have you been putting your life on hold for a paycheck? When was the last time you went after one of your cherished dreams?

_____

_____

157

_____

_____

If there was no chance that you would fail, what would you do? What would you become?

_____

_____

_____

_____

Flowering Into Being

Melinda Butterfield

"Lift up your eyes upon the day breaking for you. Give birth again
to the dream…Lift up your hearts. Each new hour holds new
chances for new beginnings."
- Maya Angelou

*O*n a beautiful October day, my friend Kara and I drove to our
friend Lisa's bridal shower. The sun was shining, the sky was an
expansive blue, and the air was crisp and cool as the gorgeous rusts
and reds of the fall season streamed by. I was very excited to share this
day with Lisa and all of the friends gathered in her honor.

As Lisa opened her gifts, I eagerly volunteered to create her paper plate
"bow bonnet" out of the bounty of ribbons, tissue, and festive trimmings
that adorned her presents. The bonnet was quite unique and pretty, and
my friends commented on my artistic abilities. Someone suggested that
I make some sort of business out of my bow bonnet creations.

159

That day, an entrepreneurial spark was ignited. Like the cracking of a
door that reveals a sliver of light, a vision had been awakened within me.
Up until that moment, I'd been perfectly content in my small massage
therapy practice, raising our three beautiful children and managing our
household. Life was full and fulfilling, and I was grateful. That simple
suggestion at Lisa's bridal shower was like a seed planted in my soul,
and it set me on a journey of great self-discovery.

Driving home with Kara, I declared, "I want to start a business that
will create financial freedom for my family. I want this so my husband
can have the space to share his talents, and do something that really
feeds his soul." My husband, Paul, is a devoted husband and father, a
thoughtful friend, an inspired philosopher, a healer, and a musician. He

has worked diligently to create a beautiful home for us, and afforded us many great luxuries and experiences. While he is successful in his real estate business, it is in his background as an acupuncturist and his affinity for ministering wisdom that I really see his amazing spirit shine.

On a mission, I explored the possibility of the bow bonnet business. I spent several weeks dreaming up a "how-to" booklet for wedding and baby showers, and researched the history of the bow bonnet. In the end, it all seemed a bit frivolous and silly; the idea was cute, but as a mom of three I had to choose wisely where to devote my energy.

Even after I shelved the bow bonnet idea, I still felt ripe and ready to burst with creative endeavoring. A few months later, a friend gifted me with a bag of the world's healthiest whole raw food. I fell in love with the food, and after a month's time, I called him to say, "I need another bag!"

"Well, Melinda," he said, "all you have to do is sign up."

Until that moment, I had not had any exposure to the industry of network marketing. I thought it was a brilliant business model; it promised the possibility of financial freedom, and was in alignment with my intentions to help heal humanity. In my massage therapy practice of fifteen years, good nutrition advice had become an integral part of my services, and I was tremendously excited to share this food with everyone I knew.

I had some success in my business, enrolling a handful of folks into my organization, gaining a few customers, and gifting bag upon bag of this food to my friends and family. It was not long before I discovered, however, that a person has to be in the right place at the right time to effectively integrate a product or business like this into their lives. There are many factors involved, and I was much better at giving the food away than actually following up with people. I made a valiant attempt to embrace the discomfort and challenges I was experiencing, and decided to focus on online marketing. Here, I could speak to an audience that was actively looking for good sources of nutrition and ways to support their livelihood in a health-conscious way.

The web learning curve was pretty steep, and simultaneously very exciting. I made some wonderful friendships and got a fabulous internet marketing education—but all of the energy I was putting forth wasn't yielding many tangible results. I was getting better at following up with prospects and jumping through all the right hoops, but I couldn't seem to catch a break. To complicate matters, I had a sneaking suspicion that there was something else, something more, that I needed to be doing.

I'd been spending most of my time talking with folks about the business opportunity offered by this food product, and sharing information to that end. However, I had a insistent, nagging feeling that something was not quite right; it was as though I was repeatedly being turned in the opposite direction. This was intolerable to me. I'd invested a lot of time and energy in my business, and I was determined to be successful!

161

Eventually, though, I had to listen to the persistent communication of Spirit. Changing my course wasn't an easy pill to swallow. Initially, I felt guilty, like I was giving up, and I fought it kicking and screaming. I broke down in my husband's arms the night I told him that I would no longer be pursuing network marketing full time. He simply held me and said, "Sometimes, we discover who we are by experiencing who we are not."

Those words resonated deeply within me. The whole reason I had started on this path was to make room for him to live into his calling. Now, I was being called upon to do the same for myself. I needed to look at who I was; at my strengths, and the gifts I had to share.

Soon after that, I traveled to a sales and marketing conference. I had a couple of business ideas brewing in my mind. The one I thought I would pursue involved business branding, and helping people to create businesses in line with the wholehearted expression of who they are. But after the leader of the conference said, "If there is something you are resisting, you need to look at it," I realized that my authentic path lay in my second idea.

Before entering into the world of network marketing, I'd set an arbitrary boundary to "not get involved" in another business that centered on nurturing people. Tending to others comes naturally to me and has brought me great joy, but because I had already spent so much of my life in this zone—with my family, in my practice, and with my friends—I decided it was time to do something different. It never occurred to me that I was keeping myself from the full expression of who I am in life and what I am here to share.

At that conference, after accepting and re-embracing my nature to nurture, I made the decision to create a business supporting pregnant women in their choice of natural childbirth. My experience of birthing each of my three children without drugs or medical intervention, the skills I have developed in my healing practice, and my love for life and people have come together into a marvelous manifestation of my gifts. Once I gained this awareness, everything just clicked. I felt like I was home.

My children's births were all significant and profound, and the labor and delivery of my middle daughter, Lucy, was an especially beautiful event. I employed a flowering visualization and self-hypnosis technique that allowed me to be in harmony with the process of birthing. The whole experience was so peaceful that few people even recognized that I was in labor. Lucy was asleep when she emerged into the world.

As I birth my business, I am employing these techniques, as well as the practices of meditation and mindfulness to encourage a sense of peace and belief within myself. Additionally, my connection to Spirit is deeply nourishing and gives me great perspective as I ride the waves of tremendous excitement and uncertainty. I can gently acknowledge my fears, and move forward in faith, trusting that as I do I will be met with the support I need and the success I desire.

I believe that we have a wonderful opportunity to flower into being when we fully engage in the dance of life. We can courageously embrace our blessings and challenges as we welcome the expression of our unique gifts. As I honor my strengths and remain true to my authentic, nurturing nature, I can consciously choose to live and work from a place that will positively impact the world while making my heart sing.

I invite you to join me.

TUNE IN TO YOUR *Authentic* SELF

The idea for a bow bonnet business is what Melinda calls a "seed thought." Have you ever pursued a seed thought to its conclusion? Where did it lead you? What evolved from it?

_____

_____

_____

_____

Starting on a path to create freedom for her husband, Melinda found it for herself. Have you ever wished for something for someone else, and then found that the wish was for you as well?

_____

_____

_____

_____

When creating your work or career path, are you integrating your gifts, or pushing them aside? How can you bring more authenticity to the work you do?

CHAPTER EIGHT

_____

_____

_____

_____

MAKING THE
Connection

The Five-Year Plan

Jennifer Longmore

*A*s a child, I wasn't exactly like the others. I was born with a "knowingness," and had a profound sense that there was something out there that was bigger than me.

Although I was reading and writing by age three, I didn't have the language skills to discuss this "knowingness" with my parents. Sometimes, I would call my mother into my room and explain to her that I saw things floating around my bed—but she couldn't see them because when she opened the door, they were gone. On certain nights, my body would expand, and I found myself floating through different dimensions, filled with a soaring energy. Back at home, I'd shrink down to a normal size and watch my teddy bears take flight, or pennies float around in the air.

My parents soon began to realize that I wasn't your average little girl— but deep down it wasn't such a surprise: like mother, like daughter. My parents were very spiritual people. My mother's father used to solve crimes for his local police department using his psychic skills. Sometimes, he would stay over at our house, and have fascinating metaphysical discussions with me, his little granddaughter. "Tell me about this," he would say. "What are you thinking now?"

As I got older, I realized that I was telekinetic. When I met people, I felt like I was watching a movie. I would ask myself, "Why is she making that decision? What is he doing?" I felt like a mini-adult in a child's body. Of course, I repressed this in the schoolyard because it was clear that I was different. Later, I dulled myself down even more.

167

I didn't follow a straight path toward a conscious life. In fact, it took an almost fatal car crash and an extremely stressful job working in child welfare to lead me to a place where I could follow my heart and truly acknowledge my gifts.

The crash took place on a bitterly cold January day, on a highway outside my college town, when I was twenty-one years old. I'd been living life in high gear, working myself into the ground, and there was no break in sight: I was on my way home for a weekend that was jam packed with activities. I would see my parents, visit my boyfriend, and hopefully do a load of laundry or two.

I merged onto a jammed six-lane highway. Everyone was whizzing by at breakneck speeds. I'd only been on the road for a few miles when a white van pulled out in front of me. The driver lost control and smashed into my bumper. My car began to rock violently from side to side. I was headed right into oncoming traffic. No one could survive that kind of impact.

All of a sudden, my car flew into reverse. The guardrail I slammed into miraculously held the weight of my car, preventing me from plunging into a deep ravine. Somehow, I was even able to guide my car off to the side of the road where, minutes later, a tow truck came to find me.

I knew for certain that this was divine intervention. That crash introduced me to the energetic side of spirituality, and would eventually re-chart my whole path.

Right after the accident, a major storm hit, but I was determined to get home. I couldn't see a thing beyond the windshield of my rental car. Gripping the wheel for dear life, I prayed. "Please let me get home safely. I will change my life. I won't do ten things at the same time anymore, or work myself into the ground. I'll pay attention to what really matters!"

All I could see was white light. It was as if my world became a blank slate, just waiting for me to write on it. I had no choice but to surrender, and trust. In my blindness, I found clarity.

The next day, my mom did some reflexology on me, and her friend did a bit of Reiki, which I found has amazing healing powers. As I was being treated, I had a huge download: not only was I going to take a Reiki class, I was going to teach it one day.

But first, I had to go back to school, and follow the conventional plans I'd set in motion. I'd invested a lot of time and money in this direction, and at the time, I didn't realize that I could actually create my own unique career path.

After graduation, I got a job as a social worker in the trenches. This step made sense to me, since many of my previous jobs had been social work related, and I'd always known that my purpose here was to help others remove the blocks that keep them from being who they really are.

169

My job was a tough one, investigating severe cases of child abuse. It was an interesting, although "secret," bonus to have someone with my skills confronting people who could abuse little ones and then (try to) lie about it. I was a witness to everything bleak and sad in that job: addiction, murder, sexual abuse. What I learned about the ins and outs of human nature would help me when I stepped into my true calling years later, but the cases I worked weighed heavily upon me. I was just too sensitive, emotionally and energetically, to do the job.

When I was offered an opportunity to go into the corporate world as a social worker dealing with employee relations and sexual harassment investigations, I jumped at it. It was a nine-to-five, no-stress job; not fulfilling in the larger sense, but at least I no longer had to make those home visits that broke my heart.

The two years I spent in the corporate world provided me the time and space I needed to allow the toxicity of my former job to seep away. While I was working with those children, I realized, fulfilling my true mission was impossible, because I was in a state of exhaustion all the time. My new position didn't demand anywhere near as much energy, and now that I had my nights free, I was able to shift my focus to my dream: becoming a healer, and opening my own business.

I started by offering energy work, Reiki, Chakra balancing, and intuitive readings. One client easily became two, and then three. Most people came to me wanting to "just feel some balance." They were suffering from myriad health concerns, stress, low energy, or unhappy marriages. During our sessions, the energy they felt would give them what they needed. They told me they felt marvelous when we finished.

At first, it was just friends and family who came to see me, but although I asked my clients not to give my name and number to anyone who wasn't a friend or relative, my client list grew rapidly. Soon, I was turning people away, because there simply weren't enough hours in the day.

I decided to conduct classes, so I could serve more people. I invited twenty to thirty participants to what became highly coveted sessions in my living room. Four times a week, I opened the doors to my home for energy healing circles. The waiting lists for these events flowed off the page.

In the beginning, all of my healing work was done on the QT, because I didn't think that my corporate bosses would understand what I did in my spare time. But this felt inauthentic because, although I was helping others to speak their truth, I wasn't speaking mine. Was it time to take the leap of faith, and do what I loved full time?

In a way, that leap was like entering that white-out zone: I was once again driving white-knuckled through the blizzard, praying I'd make it safely. This time, though, I knew I'd see a clearing.

I began marketing my services, and stepped into the energy of wonder and adventure. I made a five-year plan, laying out goals and milestones. I attracted an abundance of clients and opportunities, and embraced each of them wholeheartedly.

What I'd imagined would take five years to achieve took less than four months. Eventually, I grew my healing practice into an international business with four satellite offices, trained team members, many publications, and an acclaimed radio show.

Today, I continue to stay in a place of adventure in my business, and say "yes" to all of the opportunities that allow me to feel authentic in how I'm serving. I've learned that the more I do this, the more flow and ease I experience, and the more balanced my life is. Even when things seem unclear, I follow the white light, and know that as long as I remain authentic, I will be blessed, fulfilled, and unconditionally supported.

171

TUNE IN TO YOUR *Authentic* SELF

Did you have experiences as a child or young adult that were "out of the ordinary?" What did they mean to you then, and how do you view them now?

_____

_____

_____

_____

Jennifer's experience in her car accident changed the way she viewed her life. Have you ever had an experience in which you were required to completely let go and trust?

_____

_____

_____

_____

While still working in her corporate job, Jennifer felt "inauthentic," because she was concealing her work and true calling from her employers. Do you feel the need to hide your authentic pursuits? Why?

_____

_____

_____

_____

Angels, Animals, and Awareness

Adriana C. Tomasino

*A*fter what felt like a jolt of lightning, I found myself surrounded by real and stuffed animals, each strapped in and suspended in mid-air upon a levitating carousel. When the spinning stopped, I disembarked at a deserted and run-down area of town. The destination resembled the ruins of an ancient civilization, or perhaps the set from an episode of *The Twilight Zone*. The only familiar face swimming in this sea of the unknown was that of my beloved angelic dog, Cindy, who had made her transition almost ten years earlier. Following a brief reunion, she gestured for me to travel with her. It felt as if an eternity had passed, and yet we continued along a labyrinthine path. My canine protectress (whose namesake Cynthia is the Goddess of the Moon and the hunt, as well as the champion of children and animals), kept unseen dangers away. Then, in the blink of an eye, we bid our farewells—and I was abruptly returned to the land of the living.

173

This was only one of the many encounters I had with the other side, however brief, with increasingly pertinent messages.

A year later, my cherished dog, Coco, was in the ICU at the local animal hospital for the fifth time in a month, with no diagnosis forthcoming, and no noticeable improvement in his condition. My parents and I were devastated by his absence in our home. One night, my soul-self took an evening sojourn a few feet from where my physical body was in an apparent state of rest (or perhaps more correctly, unrest). Suddenly, I felt the presence of a Labrador retriever, whom I sensed to be Coco's Guardian. My heart sank at his appearance, as I recognized him as the harbinger of my most dreaded fear.

Soon after, upon the bittersweet occasion of my birthday, I received a card with an image bearing a striking resemblance to the Lab that figured in my nightly travels. To add to my trepidation further, during one of my family's daily visits to Coco at the hospital, another Lab came into view. He was permitted to walk around the unit, as he had been recovering from an injury. To my astonishment, he came directly to me, in sight of Coco, as if to allay my fears and ease my sorrow, while simultaneously acting as an ambassador—within hours, accompanying Coco to the Rainbow Bridge.

There was no denying these cryptic communiqués from beyond any longer. They were an unmistakable sign of my connection with the other side. All I had to do now was decipher them.

These missives from another dimension weighed heavily on my mind, especially since I always have had a fascination for that which is not easily perceived—a miraculous, mystical realm inhabited by angels, faeries, unicorns, and dragons. Synchronicity abounds in such a place, and I was ready to revisit it. After Coco's death, I felt as if I had reached a crossroads in my spiritual growth, and, within the ethers, could discern a shift in the energy around me. I was versed in multiple healing modalities and had done much inner work, but it had been years since things had flowed as effortlessly as they had when I was a child. Now, I knew I was being guided in a specific direction—but which one? It was time for Fortune's Wheel to turn again.

I started thinking back to the many dreams and visions I had witnessed that began around the age of four. As I played these films back in my mind—first of angels and otherworldly subjects, and more recently of occurrences related to my life situation and animal messengers—I realized that each vision added a new facet to my understanding. When taken in sequence, they told a story, but one that needed interpretation. As I pieced together the various fragments, their meaning became more transparent.

174

As a result of their increasing relevance to my circumstances at that time, these visions became a unquestionable signal for me to enhance my "energetic education" in earnest. Until then, I had spent most of my career in academia, which appeared to possess the keys to my calling. However, with these gentle reminders, it became evident that this was not where my heart's desire resided. I faithfully attended workshops and lectures by some of the leading metaphysical experts of our New Age: Drs. Doreen Virtue, Sonia Choquette, and Wayne Dyer, as well as Beryl Bender Birch and Hollister Rand. I also studied with local leaders of note, like Karen Noe of Angel Quest, Rev. Nina Roe of AngelsTeach, and Rev. Maria Kramer of the Awaken Peace and Love Center. With each passing day, my angels and guides, both ethereal and human, began making themselves more perceptible to me. I realized that their counsel would provide me my best chance of living authentically, from the heart, and embracing my true purpose on this planet.

Further validation arrived when I was asked to select shells from *Ocean Oracle* as part of a class assignment by its creator, my teacher and dearest friend, Michelle "Shelley" Hanson. I had studied this method of divination in depth, with ever-positive results, and was convinced about the wholly accurate and insightful nature of the wisdom communicated by the seashells. However, nothing could prepare me for the information I was about to hear from Shelley, the "shell with the voice!"

Every portion of the reading brought me to a level of awareness heretofore unachieved, but one shell in particular resonated to a greater extent than the others. I was not at all surprised at its emergence, but had to smile when Shelley conveyed the meaning of the Victor Dan's Latiaxis, which denotes a "love of pets and animals." She explained that this shell appealed to me because my life purpose involves working with the shells—these seemingly lifeless yet energetically sound organisms—as they, too, continue to exude the life force of the mollusks they once housed, just as their mammalian brothers and sisters had in their own corporeal reality. "Please consider that this shell attracted your attention for a reason," she said. Of course! These "angels of the sea" are animals, too—and they sensed my interest in learning their language and sharing their knowledge with the world.

In that instant, I *remembered*!

Shelley's astute observations evoked memories from years before, when several astrologers and psychics informed me that I possess an extraordinary bond with animals and have the ability to converse telepathically with them. I was no stranger to communicating with my own pets that way, so it would not be difficult for me to apply that gift to speak with the shells. Each shell, like every animal, is gifted with its own personality—but one untouched by the essence of ego. As Shelley teaches, the shells speak directly to the soul in an unconditionally loving manner, while offering a safe haven for the individual's needs to be addressed, so long as he or she is open to acknowledging them.

In the ensuing months, I received additional confirmation that I was getting closer to finding my true vocation. In a reading obtained via the internet, Cindy, Coco, and Grimmy (another of my dearly departed pets) provided supporting evidence for my path—in case I had not heeded their previous guidance, and the whispers of my soul. All I needed to do in order to be in greater alignment with my spirit was to figure out how to blend my affection for animals, including seashells, with my love of angels and all things numinous.

At that moment, I decided that if I were ever to live an authentic life, the time to do so was *now*!

As always, I consulted with my divine entourage, and in a flash of inspiration, the answer came to me. How had I not seen it before? It was clear as crystal. Like a charmed caduceus vibrating with the rhythm of cosmic consciousness, I could unite the enchanted communications from the heavens with the magic of the oceanic realms into the channeled readings I had already been conducting for clients.

Limitless potential and infinite possibilities lie ahead, as Fortune's Wheel has indeed come full circle, and I am finally able to embrace my authentic self!

TUNE IN TO YOUR
Authentic SELF

Do you feel a deeper-than-usual connection to animals, plants, or other living things? What can you learn from this connection?

_____

_____

_____

_____

Have you ever had a vision or dream in which you communicate with a departed loved one? What did that dream show you?

_____

_____

_____

_____

Do your dreams contain messages? Do you know what they are? Do you listen to them?

_____

_____

_____

_____

Finding Beauty

Michelle Phillips

*F*rom as far back as I can remember, I wanted to be a celebrity makeup artist. Long before it was an actual career choice or the subject of hours of reality shows, I dreamed of nothing more than powdering and primping the stars of television and film to help them be their most beautiful.

After years of getting Barbie ready for her walk down the red carpet, and having worked a stint behind the makeup counter at Bloomie's, I got my shot.

When I moved to Florida, I found out that there was a position open at the local CBS affiliate in Tampa—and I wasn't going to let a little thing like experience or a resumé get in my way, I went down and applied. Upon being asked if I could do the job, without hesitation, I said, "Of course!" I had enough trust in myself to believe that the old "fake it 'til you make it" principle applied to me—and it did. Off I went, living my dream in ways that I never thought possible.

With a little on-the-job training, I was actually pretty good. There were some interesting parts of the job, though, that you just don't learn in years of working on your dolls. The first thing I figured out was how to accentuate the most beautiful features of each individual to capture and highlight their unique qualities. The next was that, while the majority of my time was spent doing makeup, a good portion of the job was also spent counseling the people in my chair. Like a hairstylist or a bartender, I was an eager ear for the people who plopped down in my makeup room and spilled their lives out.

179

There I was, living my goal of helping others look and feel perfect. At first glance, all of my other dreams looked like they were coming true too—but something was missing in my life, and I didn't know what it was. I sensed that while I might want everything I had, I didn't have everything I wanted. That nagging sense of emptiness and longing would hang over me until the news director at the TV station where I worked offered me an opportunity that would change my life forever.

I was asked to step in front of the camera as a beauty and style correspondent to find the latest tips that could help women look and feel better. As nervous as I was, this was a very appealing offer, because my instincts told me that these were answers I needed for myself.

While researching these stories, I met women who were beautiful beyond anything I'd ever seen. They weren't models or actresses; they were women from all walks of life. And they weren't stunning because of their features, but because they were in touch with their purposes, passions, and dreams, and living them all according to their core values. The inner strength they all showed to live so uniquely and authentically had them radiating a beauty that could not be matched.

One of the most remarkable groups of women I featured invited me to join one of their workshops to learn what I later discovered was called "Life Coaching." I was instantly hooked! As this new world helped me unlock things within myself, I started to notice that a lot of the methods that life coaches used to help their clients were the same methods I'd used to help people in my makeup chair. I thought "Maybe that is what I should be doing: helping others."

A stronger instinct told me I needed to fix myself first. It was time to use these tools to change my *own* life.

Using the principles I was learning in the "coaching circles," I reclaimed my sense of purpose and passion. I rediscovered my own values—not just the values given to me by the people I was polling.

I learned to trust the answers inside me and value my own belief system. I embraced the power of my own heart, and the beauty that comes from honoring who I am. It became a part of my new purpose to share these important lessons with others, because when we honor our inner guidance system and live true to our sense of purpose, we are at our most beautiful.

The first part of reclaiming who I was and where I wanted to go was figuring out what that meant. It started out with a pretty enlightening but disturbing assessment of where I was. It turns out I was married with three beautiful children, the perfect house, the perfect car, the perfect boat…and I was miserable!

I was overworked, my kids were overscheduled, and in general I was overwhelmed. I was so consumed by trying to keep up with the Joneses and live up to everyone else's standards that I was feeling more lost by the day. I couldn't make even the simplest decisions for myself. I had become a poll-taker who needed to ask for everyone's opinion about how to raise my kids, decorate my house—even what to cook for dinner. Apparently, I had taken my time with Barbie a little too literally: I was living in the superficial world I had created.

Not to mention that, even though I was in my thirties, I was still working overtime to gain the approval of my parents and grandparents. My husband was at the top of the list of people I was constantly trying to please—but nothing I could do was right in his eyes. If I was ever going to be truly happy I was going to have to find it within.

The next thing that I learned from life coaching was that it isn't enough to know what you want: you have to take action. To reclaim the life I deserved meant that I would have to shed friends, family, and many of the material things I once thought could bring me happiness. It wasn't an easy rebuilding process. As a matter of fact, it was a living hell… for a while. I quickly found myself a divorced single mother of three. I lived on credit cards for a while, until they were maxed out; then, I turned to food stamps for survival. All of this while being offered a new job hosting a morning talk show on a top-market CBS station. So much for *rich* and famous! The job paid me less than a full time position at a fast food chain.

But there was no turning back, so I kept going *through*. I wasn't going to let fear take me down ever again. Living according to the power of my heart had given me unimaginable strength. Along with this strength came an ability to dream again, and this time I was dreaming without limits. Charting my new course, I flashed back to my days as a makeup artist, and realized that my instinctual gifts went well past just being a sounding board; I was actually good at guiding people to find their personal strengths, and empowering them to conquer difficult times in their lives.

I knew in my heart that this was my new purpose. I had made the connection between feeling beautiful and living beautifully, and it was my mission to share the process of making that connection with women everywhere. I wrote out all of the ways to do this in my journal and on my vision board, to let it be known to the Universe as clearly as possible.

Here we are, years later. Doors have flown open to make my mission a reality. I have been blessed with the opportunity to speak to up to 3,500 women at a time. I have a weekly radio show on Hay House Radio, and the book I have always dreamed of writing is going to print as I write this. It's real. Everything I ever wanted was mine for the asking—I just needed to ask!

My vision is to empower women to take action in their lives to live true to who they are, before it takes drastic measures to get them there. By doing this, I hope they can learn to be like the amazing women from my first coaching circles: powerful, free, and beautiful beyond words from the inside out.

TUNE IN TO YOUR *Authentic* SELF

What does beauty mean to you?

_____

_____

_____

_____

As Michelle learned, real beauty comes from the inside out. What helps you embrace your inner beauty? What prevents you from seeing it?

_____

183

_____

_____

_____

By trying to please other people, Michelle lost the connection to her authentic, beautiful self. Do you spend more time trying to please others than yourself? How can you shift that to honor your inner radiance?

_____

_____

_____

_____

AFTERWORD
Editor's Note

*N*ot too long ago, I attended a Zen and Yoga workshop at a local Buddhist retreat center. After a cleansing asana practice, we sat down to begin our thirty-minute seated meditation.

"You don't need to use a mantra," the instructor told us. "But if you prefer to do so, here is a simple one that a lot of our students like. As you inhale, say to yourself, 'What am I?' And as you exhale, say, 'Don't know.'"

"That's silly," my mind said. "I know who I am. I'm Bryna!"

But what is "Bryna?"

As I worked with the mantra in the quiet, my eyes started to twitch. My breath came faster; I shifted uncomfortably on my cushion. Again and again, I inhaled and asked the question, *What am I?* And with each exhale, answers popped up like corn in a kettle. I have been a teenage rebel-without-a-cause, a starving singer-songwriter with crippling stage fright, and a sassy hairstylist at an exclusive salon. I have been the founder of a successful freelance writing and design business, and the owner of a not-so-successful natural foods store. I have been the wife of a good man, and the wife of an alcoholic. (Yes, the two were one and the same.) I have been in love, and I have been divorced. I have been cynical, and I have been optimistic. I have been alone, and I have experienced the love of a beautiful, supportive community.

It wasn't long before I started to hear the underlying refrain. *I have been, I have been, I have been.* I was shocked. Was this pile of "has-beens" the foundation upon which my identity was built? Was my ego really so attached to all of the accomplishments and failures of the last thirty-two years that I couldn't step back and look at "me" as I existed in the moment? Why couldn't I examine my Self without first listing all of the qualifying factors?

Why did I need to provide a definition of "Bryna?"

I took a deep inhale, breathed it out, and for the first time was able to complete the original mantra. *Don't know.*

Randall Curtis, a nationally-renowned astrologer, writes about the "Curse of Identification" in his book, *Planetary Clusters.* Basically, when we identify with the events and relationships in our lives, past or present—when we create an identity around them—we *become* those events and relationships. By telling ourselves stories about ourselves, we take on the roles of characters in those stories, playing the parts assigned to us by our "narrator," the intellect. Only when we shift that identification (or better yet, let go of it completely) can we begin to uncover our truest, most authentic selves—the luminescent, valuable, divine, utterly human beings we are right now, in this moment.

Every one of the women in this book needed to make a shift to transform her life. Sometimes, this shift was a physical one, but more often it was a shift of *identification*. No longer content to be who they were, our authors rewrote their internal scripts to better reflect the strong, authentic women they knew they could, and *would*, become. In the mirrors of their stories, I saw fragments of myself reflected back at me. Their words jumped off the pages and into my heart, planting seeds of inspiration on days when life felt like it was all too much to handle.

The day after my divorce was finalized, I read Aimée Yawnick's story, and realized that I, too, have buried my authenticity beneath a protective, glossy exterior, to the detriment of my relationships. I saw my own insecurities at play in Lisa Marie Rosati's wake-up call, and wondered if my subversive "little liar" is in fact a close cousin to Rev. Nina Roe's. Just like Saskia Röell, I have doubted the words of my Soul, only to find that I was cared for all along. And while I have yet to experience the ecstasy of complete self-acceptance that was the beginning of Aysha Strausbaugh's miracle, I have hope that, someday, I will.

So who am I: the former wife of an alcoholic, a failed songwriter, a frightened and cynical seeker of abuse? Or am I a successful yoga instructor, writer, and editor; a confident and beautiful woman who trusts in the power of the Universe and the acknowledges the blessings that surround her every day?

Don't know—but the choice is, and has always been, mine to make. 187

Yours in gratitude,

Bryna René

Editor, Inspired Living Publishing, LLC

ABOUT OUR

Authors

Sharon Babineau

Sharon Babineau is an award winning inspirational speaker, decorated military soldier, mountain climber, hockey player, mother, and volunteer. She is the founder of a not-for-profit organization called Maddie's Everlasting Wish, named in memory of her daughter. Sharon inspires others to embrace their right to happiness, and has facilitated workshops, seminars, and support groups for over a decade. She walks her talk with a powerful story of inspiration and hope. Her story has appeared in print and on television and radio, including a feature on "No Opportunity Wasted with Phil Keoghan" (Amazing Race). Contact Sharon at sharon@mindbreak.ca or visit www. mindbreak.ca and www.maddieswishproject.com.

Melinda Butterfield

189

Melinda Butterfield is a radiant expression of God's love and light, a nationally certified massage therapist for fifteen years, and a DONA-trained Doula. A blessed mother of three and founder of the business, Encouraging Birth, Melinda helps pregnant women all over the world discover loving support, positive mindset practices and easy birthing techniques essential to experiencing more peace and confidence in their natural childbirth process. Connect with Melinda today at www.encouragingbirth.com.

Donna Cravotta

Donna Cravotta founded Virtual Management Concepts, LLC, a mom-owned business offering authors and solo and small businesses assistance with online marketing, social media management, author support, and PR services. Donna and her son live outside New York City. Find out more about Donna at www.virtualmanagementconceptsllc.com

Andra Evans

Andra Evans, BA(Hons), RIHR lives, loves, works, and plays in Toronto, Canada. An expert in the art of reinvention, Andra has been called a "midwife of the spirit" and a "soul whisperer," and is a multi-talented intuitive healer, teacher, and mentor. She uses her medicine bag of experience, wisdom, humor, energy, and gifts from the earth to help people bring light to their soul's journey and manage transformation and change. Find out more about cultivating your authentic self at www.justandra.com.

Nancy Fisher

Nancy Fisher has been mentoring people in their life transitions for the past 20 years, first through her private home care business, and now as Founder of Onward and Upward, her Life/Business coaching practice which empowers women to increase their potential to find their true life's purpose. She is a mother, grandmother, inspirational conference speaker, golfer and life enthusiast. Clients describe her as motivator, mentor, business consultant and very empowering. Visit Nancy at www.onwardandupwardscoaching.com, or e-mail nancy@onwardandupwardscoaching.com

Kari Henley

Kari Henley is a whirlwind entrepreneur, dynamic speaker, avid writer, mother of four, and active community activist. She believes the world is losing touch with one another, and is committed to inspiring connection, authenticity and growth through her innovative programs. She is the founder of Gather Central, which features interactive online events including the "Girls Around the World" Tele-Camps, a virtual book club, tele-summits, conference call workshops, online support groups, and more. She is a weekly contributor to the Huffington Post, and offers workshops or custom retreats for adults and youth on the power of creating community. Visit www.gathercentral.com or contact Kari directly at: kari@gathercentral.com.

Catrice M. Jackson

Catrice M. Jackson is recognized around the world as the Savvy, Sassy, Fearless Empowerment Speaker and Fear-Free Living Expert. She passionately pioneers her global mission to empower women to get NAKED and live their authentic truth. Through speaking, personal life coaching, consulting and her internet radio show, Catrice helps women master the Art of Fear-Free Living through *Catriceology*, the psychology of living deliciously! Find Catrice online at www.catriceologyenterprises.com.

Gayle Joplin Hall, PhD

Gayle Joplin Hall, PhD, is President and Founder of Dr. Hall on Call™ and Hall Ways to Happiness™. Gayle's doctorate is in Psychology. She is a Keynote Speaker and Expert in Domestic Violence, Crisis Analysis, and Behavior Consulting. Dr. Hall is an author, Life Coach, Professor, and entrepreneur. As The Happiness Life Coach™, she will guide you to discovering your bliss. For speaking engagements or to schedule your "Hall-Call," please visit: www.drhalloncall.com, or contact gaylehallphd@gmail.com.

Rachel Larkin

Rachel Larkin is the mother of two young boys, and lives in Wanaka, New Zealand. She is committed to enabling young people aged from five to twenty-four to develop their self-esteem through personal adventures in the outdoors. Inspired by the Law of Attraction and other self-development techniques, she continues to experience her own journey toward self-realization. Find Rachel online at larkinconsultancy@gmail.com.

Christine Laureano

Christine Laureano is an entrepreneur, Coach, and Visionary Leader who collaborates with motivated, soul-inspired women entrepreneurs to find the soul of their businesses and bring their ideas to life! With over 25 years of inspiring women as a Corporate Sales Executive, entrepreneur, parent and life coach, Christine offers fresh perspectives and ideas that move women beyond the shadow of doubt to expand their businesses and develop a rock-solid foundation for success. Find Christine online at www.christinelaureano.com, e-mail christine@christinelaureanocoaching.com, or call (631) 484-6335

Jennifer Longmore

Jennifer Longmore, North America's Soul Purpose Expert, internationally acclaimed host of "Soul Purpose Central," and best-selling author, is world-renowned for her ability to bridge the connection to universal consciousness. She is a leading expert on Akashic Records and has served thousands of souls as founder of the Soul Journeys® School for Akashic Studies and the Soul Journeys® Method. For more than 15 years, she has helped clients to permanently shift limiting beliefs and patterns that prevent them from being who they really, and allow them to live their most abundant, aligned, and accelerated soul's journey. Find Jennifer online at www.souljourneys.ca.

Carolyn McGee

As an Angelic Life Coach and Reiki Master, Carolyn McGee loves helping people to discover the joy of self-belief. She works in partnership with the angels to assist others to uncover their true passion, connect with their inner radiance and follow the path of their life purpose. Carolyn has learned from her every experience and relationship, and can guide you to find the hidden gifts in the challenging ones. To learn more, please visit www.gatewaytoyou.com.

Lisa Michaels

Celebrated elemental wisdom teacher, author, and Natural Rhythms President, Lisa Michaels, teaches you how to connect with the profound power of Nature so you can dramatically increase your ability to thrive in every area of life. Chosen as a Hay House Mover & Shaker, Lisa can help you ignite your inner gifts and create more dynamic success through her products, workshops, and facilitator and coach trainings. Download a free Natural Rhythms Starter Kit at www.naturalrhythms.org.

Cathleen O'Connor

The Balance Whisperer, aka Cathleen O'Connor, is a specialist in authentic business branding, a keynote speaker, intuitive dream analyst, life and business coach and the author of *Harriet Takes the Wheel* and *The Everything Law of Attraction Dream Dictionary*. Her CD, *From Stress to Serenity*, features guided imagery meditations for your daily life. Cathleen loves to inspire other women to act on their most cherished dreams and create lives of joy, fulfillment and success. Find Cathleen online at www.thebalancewhisperer.com.

Michelle Phillips

From live TV to live events Michelle Phillips has inspired millions! As a celebrity makeup artist and Life Coach she works with people everywhere to bring out their best from the inside out. She shares this message in her speaking programs, TV appearances, radio show on Hay House Radio, and in her new book, *The Beauty Blueprint: 8 Steps to Building the Life and Look of Your Dreams* (Hay House, 2011). Connect with Michelle at www.michellephillips.com.

Joani Plenty

Joani Plenty is a coveted speaker and motivational writer who is committed to excellence. One of her passions is inspiring others to do the same. Joani is a member of Coachville, NAFE and Women Speakers Association. She spends her spare time as a voiceover actress and singing in front of the mirror with her hairbrush microphone. Joani is currently writing a children's book, lives in NJ with her family and "Phil," the groundhog who lives under the shed. Find her at www.joaniplenty.com, or e-mail jplenty@joaniplenty.com. You can also "friend" Joani on Facebook.

Rev. Nina Roe

Rev. Nina Roe is the Founder of AngelsTeach. She discovered her life mission in her forties: to mentor and teach inspired souls how to connect with their angels and reclaim the magic of everyday life. For information about online classes, readings and the Living with the Angels™ membership program, visit www.angelsteach.com.

Saskia Röell

Saskia Röell is the connection to your Soul. Using her own life as living proof that extraordinary choices lead to an extraordinary life, she expertly helps others do the same. As a Soul Empowerment Coach, best-selling author, coauthor with Jack Canfield and Deepak Chopra, speaker, healer, and mother of five, Saskia empowers you to move out of your comfort zone, break through your fears, and go after your heart's desires. She works internationally with people from all walks of life and has successfully helped many people live their biggest dreams. Find Saskia online at www.yoursoulguidance.com and www.suitcasefulloffaith.com.

Lisa Marie Rosati

Lisa Marie Rosati is a Relationships, Life, and Wellness Expert, a certified Life and Health Coach, and an expert for Dr. Oz's website, www.sharecare.com. Her websites offer a variety of products to support you, your relationships, and your wellness. Learn more about Lisa's Life and Relationship Strategy work at www.createauthenticrelationships.com. Learn about her sure-fire ways to lose weight, feel great, and get healthy at www.threecavemenandalady.com

Kathleen E. Sims

A self-made success through a lifetime of deep inquiry and rich experience, Kathleen E. Sims, C.H.T., C.R.C., has emerged as one of the Global Leaders in the field of Love, Purpose and Creating a 'Juicy' Life. She is a coauthor of the best-selling books *Wake Up Women—BE Happy, Healthy & Wealthy, Wake Up—Moments of Inspiration* and *A Juicy, Joyful Life*, as well as a motivational speaker, Love and Spiritual life coach, trainer, and hypnotherapist. She is committed to helping others live purposeful lives filled with abiding, lasting love. Call Kathleen for a free consultation at (925) 674-9003, or check out her websites: www.lifetimeloveconnection.com, www.thewonderofwomen.com, www.liveyourvisionworkshop.com, and www.innertrails.com.

Aysha Strausbaugh

Aysha Strausbaugh is a Making Miracles: Bonding Before Birth life coach and Core Alignment Specialist, as well as an amazing hairstylist, entrepreneur, circus performer, and previous owner of Studio Catwalk Hair Salon. A member of Alcoholics Anonymous since 1989, she is a lover of dance, karaoke, family, friends, Disneyland, laughter, stories, and babies. In 2008, Aysha gave birth to her miracle daughter Chloie, proving that the impossible is possible if you just believe; hence, Making Miracles Coaching was born. Learn more at www.makingmiraclescoaching.com.

Adriana C. Tomasino

Adriana C. Tomasino is a Professional Seashell Reader of the Ocean Oracle™ system, Crystal/Energy Healer, Reiki Master Instructor, Registered Yoga Teacher, Angel Communication Specialist™ and Master, as well as Integrated Energy Therapy® Master-Instructor. She is currently a doctoral candidate in medieval literature, and cofounder/President of Heaven Seas: Wings and Harps, a business dedicated to providing individuals with the tools for empowerment through readings, healings and yoga. For more information, please visit www.wingsandharps.com or e-mail dreemstar1@yahoo.com.

Kim Turcotte

Kim Turcotte gets jazzed about helping service-based businesswomen get clear about their own passion and purpose. She helps them to uncover their Core Purpose and create a strategic plan to build their businesses around this purpose. Kim doesn't just support clients through creating a solid business strategy; she has the technical skills to support them through the implementation of that strategy. No more getting stalled mid-process! Kim and her team help clients create systems, automate their businesses, and build websites aligned with their passion and purpose! To learn more, visit Kim online at www.kimturcotte.com.

Shann Vander Leek

Shann Vander Leek: successful television advertising sales maven turned international Life on Your Terms Accelerator, yogini, and author of *Life on Your Terms*. Unconventional and delightfully curious; she is a wildly sought-after transition coach who inspires powerful executive women in transition to get focused now, follow their passion and create more balance in their lives. Accelerate your life on your terms with Shann's Signature Coaching System. Find Shann at www.shannvanderleek.com or www.truebalancelifecoaching.com.

Kati Neal Verburg

Kati Verburg is a freelance writer located in Portland, Oregon, and often writes about subjects related to self-esteem. Recognizing that her related challenges were not necessarily unique to her, she founded Truly B, a media campaign advocating a positive sense of self-worth in girls of any age. Kati is dedicated to spreading messages that inspire an awareness of self-talk, personal responsibility, the importance of choice, and all that is beautiful, brilliant, bountiful, benevolent, brave, and boundless about us! Visit Truly B at www.trulyb.com.

Aimée Yawnick

Balancing the Spiritual Laws of the Universe and practical proven tools and techniques, Aimée helps her clients achieve higher levels of confidence and self-worth so they can discover and fulfill their Divine purpose. Aimée guides the way and clears out the junk so you can easily embrace the woman you are meant to be. Grab your free copy of Aimée's revolutionary report, "Your Inner Guide To Good Fortune," at www.coregrowthanddevelopment.com/eyas.

ABOUT THE PUBLISHER

Linda Joy

L inda Joy is one of the premiere voices in women's inspirational publishing today. Following the calling of her heart, Linda lives her soul's purpose as a best-selling publisher, sought-after inspirational speaker, and Conscious Business Catalyst dedicated to inspiring women to live deeper, more authentic, inspired lives. She is passionate about helping women around the world rediscover and reconnect with their inner wisdom, and trust in the power of their dreams.

In her twenty-year journey from welfare mother to award-winning entrepreneur, Linda learned firsthand the power of passion, courage, and perseverance. She has walked the walk, and believes that there are no failures in life—only lessons to be learned and shared. Linda has been invited to share this heartfelt wisdom both at colleges and women's forums and through global virtual events such as the *100 Women of Destiny* tele-summit, where she shared the virtual platform with visionaries like Marianne Williamson, Barbara Marx Hubbard, and Mallika Chopra. As host of the *Inspired Living Secrets* tele-seminar series, twice a year Ms. Joy invites twenty-four of today's leading visionaries in the fields of personal and spiritual development, natural health, and human potential to share their wisdom with her audience. The *Authentic Conversations with Extraordinary Women* podcast series uses authentic storytelling as a tool to help women transform their lives.

With the mission to inspire women to live from the inside out, Ms. Joy founded *Aspire Magazine* in 2005. Now the premiere inspirational digital magazine for women, *Aspire* publishes six content-rich issues per year featuring today's leading visionaries, authors, and speakers, and reaches subscribers around the world. As part of her personal commitment to bring women the resources to live authentically, Linda donates free issues of *Aspire* as part of her global "Mission to Inspire 100,000 Women" campaign.

In early 2010, Linda dove deeper into the power of authentic storytelling, and Inspired Living Publishing was born. Hours after its release in September 2010, ILP's first book, the anthology *A Juicy Joyful Life,* hit #1 in Amazon's Hot New Releases in multiple categories. With the release of Embracing Your Authentic Self, Ms. Joy continues to bring women's stories to life, and in 2012 Inspired Living Publishing will move toward publishing full-length works by women authors in the inspirational genre.

To Learn More about Linda Joy – visit www.linda-joy.com, Twitter: @LindaJoy
To Claim your Free Subscription to Aspire Magazine – visit www.subscribetoaspire.com
To Tune in to Inspired Living Secrets – visit www.inspiredlivingsecrets.com
To Listen to Authentic Conversations – visit www.authenticconversationswithlinda.com
To receive updates on upcoming publishing projects – visit www.inspiredlivingpiblishing.com

ABOUT THE EDITOR
Bryna René

*B*ryna René is an accomplished freelance writer and editor dedicated to helping entrepreneurs, visionaries, and spiritual beings around the world bring their messages to light through online and print media.

The editor of *A Juicy Joyful Life*, the first best-selling anthology from Inspired Living Publishing, Bryna has also coauthored and edited numerous successful non-fiction books, and her short fiction has placed in several national and international competitions.

When she's not lovingly molding the written word, Bryna builds websites for holistic businesses. She also teaches Vinyasa and Prana Flow® yoga through weekly classes and workshops at studios across Rhode Island and the U.S.

Find Bryna on the web at www.wordsbyaphrodite.com and www.brynarene.com.
Contact her at (401) 339-1944 or bryna@wordsbyaphrodite.com.

197

INSPIRED LIVING PUBLISHING, LLC

...Inspiring the world, one word at a time.

Inspired Living Publishing, LLC is dedicated to publishing inspirational stories, titles, and authors whose messages have the power to transform and enhance the lives of others.

At **Inspired Living Publishing, LLC**, we are passionate about providing traditional and non-traditional publishing opportunities which allow women to share their wisdom, stories, and insights with other women across the globe.

At **Inspired Living Publishing, LLC** we believe in the power of the written word to transform lives.

Share Your *Wisdom* in One of Our
Upcoming Projects!

Sign up for our ILP Newsletter for project announcements:
www.InspiredLivingPublishing.com

PO Box 1149 | Lakeville, MA 02347